Michael Ondaatje

The Cinnamon Peeler

Michael Ondaatje is a novelist and poet who lives in Toronto, Canada. He is the author of *The English Patient*, *In the Skin of a Lion*, *Coming Through Slaughter*, and *The Collected Works of Billy the Kid*; two other collections of poems, *Secular Love* and *There's a Trick with a Knife I'm Learning to Do*; and a memoir, *Running in the Family*. He received the Booker Prize for *The English Patient*.

VINTAGE

INTERNATIONAL

BOOKS BY Michael Ondaatje

PROSE

The English Patient
1992

In the Skin of a Lion
1987

Running in the Family (memoir)
1982

Coming Through Slaughter
1976

The Collected Works of Billy the Kid
1970

POETRY

The Cinnamon Peeler: Selected Poems
1991

Secular Love
1984

There's a Trick with a Knife
I'm Learning to Do: Poems 1963–1978
1979

The Cinnamon Peeler

Selected Poems

January, 2001

For Sal:

These are the things I have in my heart.
Heart and skills, there's nothing else.

(p. 167)

Except movies!

Happy birthday —

love,
Fredda

The Cinnamon Peeler

Selected Poems

Michael Ondaatje

VINTAGE INTERNATIONAL

Vintage Books

A Division of Random House, Inc.   New York

FIRST VINTAGE INTERNATIONAL EDITION, JANUARY 1997

Copyright © 1989, 1991 by Michael Ondaatje

All rights reserved under International and Pan-American
Copyright Conventions. Published in the United States by Vintage
Books, a division of Random House, Inc., New York. Originally
published in slightly different form in Great Britain by
Pan Books Ltd., London, in hardcover in 1989 and subsequently
in the United States by Alfred A. Knopf, Inc., New York,
in hardcover in 1991, and in paperback in 1992.
Published simultaneously in Canada by McClelland
and Stewart, Inc., Toronto.

Most of the poems in this collection were originally published
in *There's a Trick with a Knife I'm Learning to Do* (1979) and
Secular Love (1984), published by W. W. Norton & Company, Inc.
Copyright © 1979 by Michael Ondaatje
Copyright © 1984 by Michael Ondaatje

The Library of Congress has cataloged
the Knopf edition(s) as follows:
Ondaatje, Michael, 1943–
The cinnamon peeler : poems / Michael Ondaatje.—1st ed.
p. cm.
ISBN 0-679-40260-8 (Knopf hardcover)
ISBN 0-679-74272-7 (Knopf paperback)
I. Title.
PR9199.3.O5C5 1991
811'.54—dc20 90-53557
CIP

Vintage ISBN: 0-679-77913-2

Author photograph © Dominic Sansoni

Printed in the United States of America
10 9 8 7 6

For Barrie Nichol

Contents

There's a trick
with a knife
I'm learning to do

'Deep colour and big, shaggy nose. Rather a jumbly, untidy sort of wine, with fruitiness shooting off one way, firmness another, and body pushing about underneath. It will be as comfortable and comforting as the 1961 Nuits St Georges when it has pulled its ends in and settled down.'

MAGAZINE DESCRIPTION OF A WINE

LIGHT

for Doris Gratiaen

Midnight storm. Trees walking off across the fields in fury
naked in the spark of lightning.
I sit on the white porch on the brown hanging cane chair
coffee in my hand midnight storm midsummer night.
The past, friends and family, drift into the rain shower.
Those relatives in my favourite slides
re-shot from old minute photographs so they now stand
complex ambiguous grainy on my wall.

This is my Uncle who turned up for his marriage
on an elephant. He was a chaplain.
This shy looking man in the light jacket and tie was infamous,
when he went drinking he took the long blonde beautiful hair
of his wife and put one end in the cupboard and locked it
leaving her tethered in an armchair.
He was terrified of her possible adultery
and this way died peaceful happy to the end.
My Grandmother, who went to a dance in a muslin dress
with fireflies captured and embedded in the cloth, shining
and witty. This calm beautiful face
organized wild acts in the tropics.
She hid the milkman in her house
after he had committed murder and at the trial
was thrown out of the court for making jokes at the judge.
Her son became a Q.C.
This is my brother at 6. With his cousin and his sister
and Pam de Voss who fell on a penknife and lost her eye.
My Aunt Christie. She knew Harold Macmillan was a spy
communicating with her through pictures in the newspapers.
Every picture she believed asked her to forgive him,
his hound eyes pleading.

Her husband, Uncle Fitzroy, a doctor in Ceylon,

had a memory sharp as scalpels into his 80's,
though I never bothered to ask him about anything
 – interested then more in the latest recordings of Bobby Darin.

And this is my Mother with her brother Noel in fancy dress.
They are 7 and 8 years old, a hand-coloured photograph,
it is the earliest picture I have. The one I love most.
A picture of my kids at Halloween
has the same contact and laughter.
My Uncle dying at 68, and my Mother a year later dying at 68.
She told me about his death and the day he died
his eyes clearing out of illness as if seeing
right through the room the hospital and she said
he saw something so clear and good his whole body
for a moment became youthful and she remembered
when she sewed badges on his trackshirts.
Her voice joyous in telling me this, her face light and clear.
(My firefly Grandmother also dying at 68).

These are the fragments I have of them, tonight
in this storm, the dogs restless on the porch.
They were all laughing, crazy, and vivid in their prime.
At a party my drunk Father
tried to explain a complex operation on chickens
and managed to kill them all in the process, the guests
having dinner an hour later while my Father slept
and the kids watched the servants clean up the litter
of beaks and feathers on the lawn.

These are their fragments, all I remember,
wanting more knowledge of them. In the mirror and in my kids
I see them in my flesh. Wherever we are
they parade in my brain and the expanding stories
connect to the grey grainy pictures on the wall,
as they hold their drinks or 20 years later
hold grandchildren, pose with favourite dogs,
coming through the light, the electricity, which the storm
destroyed an hour ago, a tree going down by the highway
so that now inside the kids play dominoes by candlelight
and out here the thick rain static the spark of my match
                                    to a cigarette
and the trees across the fields leaving me, distinct
lonely in their own knife scars and cow-chewed bark
frozen in the jagged light as if snapped in their run
the branch arms waving to what was a second ago the dark sky
when in truth like me they haven't moved.
Haven't moved an inch from me.

EARLY MORNING, KINGSTON
TO GANANOQUE

The twenty miles to Gananoque
with tangled dust blue grass
burned, and smelling burned
along the highway
is land too harsh for picnics.
Deep in the fields
behind stiff dirt fern
nature breeds the unnatural.

Escaping cows canter white
then black and white
along the median, forming out of mist.
Crows pick at animal accidents,
with swoops lift meals—
blistered groundhogs, stripped snakes
to arch behind a shield of sun.

Somewhere in those fields
they are shaping new kinds of women.

A HOUSE DIVIDED

This midnight breathing
heaves with no sensible rhythm,
is fashioned by no metronome.
Your body, eager
for the extra yard of bed,
reconnoitres and outflanks;
I bend in peculiar angles.

This nightly battle is fought with subtleties:
you get pregnant, I'm sure,
just for extra ground
 — immune from kicks now.

Inside you now's another,
thrashing like a fish,
swinging, fighting
for its inch already.

THE DIVERSE CAUSES

for than all erbys and treys renewyth a man and woman,
and in lyke wyse lovers callyth to their mynde olde
jantylnes and olde servyse, and many kynde dedes that
was forgotyn by necylgence

Three clouds and a tree
reflect themselves on a toaster.
The kitchen window hangs scarred,
shattered by winter hunters.

We are in a cell of civilized magic.
Stravinsky roars at breakfast,
our milk is powdered.

Outside, a May god
moves his paws to alter wind
to scatter shadows of tree and cloud.
The minute birds walk confident
jostling the cold grass.
The world not yet of men.

We clean buckets of their sand
to fetch water in the morning,
reach for winter cobwebs,
sweep up moths who have forgotten to waken.
When the children sleep, angled
behind their bottles, you can hear mice prowl.

I turn a page
careful not to break the rhythms
of your sleeping head on my hip,
watch the moving under your eyelid
that turns like fire,
and we have love and the god outside
until ice starts to limp
in brown hidden waterfalls,
or my daughter burns the lake
by reflecting her red shoes in it.

SIGNATURE

The car carried him
racing the obvious moon
beating in the trees like a white bird.

Difficult to make words sing
around your appendix.
The obvious upsets me,
everyone has scars which crawl
into the mystery of swimming trunks.

I was the first appendix in my family.
My brother who was given the stigma
of a rare blood type
proved to have ulcers instead.

The rain fell like applause as I approached the hospital.

It takes seven seconds she said,
strapped my feet,
entered my arm.
I stretched all senses
on *five*
the room closed on me like an eyelid.

At night the harmonica plays,
a whistler joins in respect.
I am a sweating marble saint
full of demerol and sleeping pills.
A man in the armour of shining plaster
walks to my door, then past.
Imagine the rain
falling like white bees on the sidewalk
imagine Snyder
high on poetry and mountains

Three floors down
my appendix
swims in a jar.

O world, I shall be buried all over Ontario

HENRI ROUSSEAU AND FRIENDS
for Bill Muysson

In his clean vegetation
the parrot, judicious,
poses on a branch.
The narrator of the scene,
aware of the perfect fruits,
the white and blue flowers,
the snake with an ear for music;
he presides.

The apes
hold their oranges like skulls,
like chalices.
They are below the parrot
above the oranges—
a jungle serfdom which
with this order
reposes.

They are the ideals of dreams.
Among the exactness,
the symmetrical petals,
the efficiently flying angels,
there is complete liberation.
The parrot is interchangeable;
tomorrow in its place
a waltzing man and tiger,
brash legs of a bird.

Greatness achieved
they loll among textbook flowers
and in this pose hang
scattered like pearls
in just as intense a society.
On Miss Adelaide Milton de Groot's walls,
with Lillie P. Bliss in New York.

And there too
in spangled wrists and elbows
and grand façades of cocktails
are vulgarly beautiful parrots, appalled lions,
the beautiful and the forceful locked in suns,
and the slight, careful stepping birds.

APPLICATION FOR A DRIVING LICENCE

Two birds loved
in a flurry of red feathers
like a burst cottonball,
continuing while I drove over them.

I am a good driver, nothing shocks me.

THE TIME AROUND SCARS

A girl whom I've not spoken to
or shared coffee with for several years
writes of an old scar.
On her wrist it sleeps, smooth and white,
the size of a leech.
I gave it to her
brandishing a new Italian penknife.
Look, I said turning,
and blood spat onto her shirt.

My wife has scars like spread raindrops
on knees and ankles,
she talks of broken greenhouse panes
and yet, apart from imagining red feet,
(a nymph out of Chagall)
I bring little to that scene.
We remember the time around scars,
they freeze irrelevant emotions
and divide us from present friends.
I remember this girl's face,
the widening rise of surprise.

And would she
moving with lover or husband
conceal or flaunt it,
or keep it at her wrist
a mysterious watch.
And this scar I then remember
is medallion of no emotion.

I would meet you now
and I would wish this scar
to have been given with
all the love
that never occurred between us.

FOR JOHN, FALLING

Men stopped in the heel of sun,
hum of engines evaporated;
the machine displayed itself bellied with mud
and balanced – immense.

No one ran to where
his tensed muscles curled unusually,
where jaws collected blood,
the hole in his chest the size of fists,
hands clutched to eyes like a blindness.

Arched there he made
ridiculous requests for air.
And twelve construction workers
what should they do but surround
or examine the path of falling.

And the press in bright shirts,
a doctor, the foreman scuffing a mound,
men removing helmets,
the machine above him
shielding out the sun
while he drowned
in the dark orgasm of his mouth.

THE GOODNIGHT

With the bleak heron Paris
imagine Philoctetes
the powerful fat-thighed man,
the bandaged smelling foot
with rivers of bloodshot veins
scattering like trails into his thighs:
a man who roared on an island for ten years,
whose body grew banal
while he stayed humane
behind the black teeth and withering hair.

Imagine in his hands – black
from the dried blood of animals,
a bow of torn silver
that noised arrows loose like a wild heart;

in front of him – Paris
darting and turning, the perfumed stag,
and beyond him the sun
netted in the hills, throwing back his shape,
until the running spider of shadow
gaped on the bandaged foot of the standing man
who let shafts of eagles into the ribs
that were moving to mountains.

PHILOCTETES ON THE ISLAND

Sun moves broken in the trees
drops like a paw
turns sea to red leopard

I trap sharks and drown them
stuffing gills with sand
cut them with coral till
the blurred grey runs
red designs.

And kill to fool myself alive
to leave all pity on the staggering body
in order not to shoot an arrow up
and let it hurl
down through my petalling skull
or neck vein, and lie
heaving round the wood in my lung.
That the end of thinking.
Shoot either eye of bird instead
and run and catch it in your hand.

One day a bird went mad
flew blind along the beach
smashed into a dropping wave
out again and plummeted.
Later knocked along the shore.

To slow an animal
you break its foot with a stone
so two run wounded
reel in the bush, flap
bodies at each other
till free of forest
it gallops broken in the sand,
then use a bow
and pin the tongue back down its throat.

With wind the rain wheels like a circus hoof,
aims at my eyes, rakes up the smell of animals
of stone moss, cleans me.
Branches fall like nightmares in the dark
till sun breaks up
and spreads wound fire at my feet

then they smell me,
the beautiful animals

ELIZABETH

Catch, my Uncle Jack said
and oh I caught this huge apple
red as Mrs Kelly's bum.
It's red as Mrs Kelly's bum, I said
and Daddy roared
and swung me on his stomach with a heave.
Then I hid the apple in my room
till it shrunk like a face
growing eyes and teeth ribs.

Then Daddy took me to the zoo
he knew the man there
they put a snake around my neck
and it crawled down the front of my dress.
I felt its flicking tongue
dripping onto me like a shower.
Daddy laughed and said Smart Snake
and Mrs Kelly with us scowled.

In the pond where they kept the goldfish
Philip and I broke the ice with spades
and tried to spear the fishes;
we killed one and Philip ate it,
then he kissed me
with raw saltless fish in his mouth.

My sister Mary's got bad teeth
and said I was lucky, then she said
I had big teeth, but Philip said I was pretty.
He had big hands that smelled.

I would speak of Tom, soft laughing,
who danced in the mornings round the sundial
teaching me the steps from France, turning
with the rhythm of the sun on the warped branches,
who'd hold my breast and watch it move like a snail
leaving his quick urgent love in my palm.
And I kept his love in my palm till it blistered.

When they axed his shoulders and neck
the blood moved like a branch into the crowd.
And he staggered with his hanging shoulder
cursing their thrilled cry, wheeling,
waltzing in the French style to his knees
holding his head with the ground,
blood settling on his clothes like a blush;
this way
when they aimed the thud into his back.

And I find cool entertainment now
with white young Essex, and my nimble rhymes.

She said, 'What about Handy? Think I should send it to him?'

'He's supposed to call in a little while. I'll ask him.'

'He retired, didn't he?'

'Yes.'

She waited and then said, 'Say something, Parker. God to get you to gossip, it's like pulling teeth.'

'Handy retired.' Parker said.

'I know he retired! Tell me about it. Tell me why he retired, tell me where he is, how's he doing. Talk to me, Parker, goddamit.'

RICHARD STARK, *The Sour Lemon Score*

DATES

It becomes apparent that I miss great occasions.
My birth was heralded by nothing
but the anniversary of Winston Churchill's marriage.
No monuments bled, no instruments
agreed on a specific weather.
It was a seasonal insignificance.

I console myself with my mother's eighth month.
While she sweated out her pregnancy in Ceylon
a servant ambling over the lawn
with a tray of iced drinks,
a few friends visiting her
to placate her shape, and I
drinking the life lines,
Wallace Stevens sat down in Connecticut
a glass of orange juice at his table
so hot he wore only shorts
and on the back of a letter
began to write 'The Well Dressed Man with a Beard'.

That night while my mother slept
her significant belly cooled
by the bedroom fan
Stevens put words together
that grew to sentences
and shaved them clean and
shaped them, the page suddenly
becoming thought where nothing had been,
his head making his hand
move where he wanted
and he saw his hand was saying
the mind is never finished, no, never
and I in my mother's stomach was growing
as were the flowers outside the Connecticut windows.

BILLBOARDS

'Even his jokes were exceedingly drastic.'

My wife's problems with husbands, houses,
her children that I meet
at stations in Kingston, in Toronto, in London Ontario
 – they come down the grey steps
bright as actors after their drugged four hour ride
of spilled orange juice and comics.
Reunions for Easter egg hunts.
Kite flying. Christmases.
All this, I was about to say,
invades my virgin past.

When she was beginning
this anthology of kids
I moved – blind but for senses
jutting *faux pas*, terrible humour,
shifted with a sea of persons,
breaking when necessary
into smaller self sufficient bits of mercury.
My mind a carefully empty diary
till I hit the barrier reef
that was my wife—
                    there
the right bright fish
among the coral.

With her came the locusts of history—
innuendoes she had missed
varied attempts at seduction
dogs who had been bred
and killed by taxis or brain disease.
Here was I trying to live
with a neutrality so great
I'd have nothing to think about.
Nowadays I get the feeling
I'm in a complex situation,
one of several billboard posters
blending in the rain.

I am writing this with a pen my wife has used
to write a letter to her first husband.
On it is the smell of her hair.
She must have placed it down between sentences
and thought, and driven her fingers round her skull
gathered the slightest smell of her head
and brought it back to the pen.

LETTERS & OTHER WORLDS

'for there was no more darkness for him and, no doubt like Adam before the fall, he could see in the dark'

My father's body was a globe of fear
His body was a town we never knew
He hid that he had been where we were going
His letters were a room he seldom lived in
In them the logic of his love could grow

My father's body was a town of fear
He was the only witness to its fear dance
He hid where he had been that we might lose him
His letters were a room his body scared

He came to death with his mind drowning.
On the last day he enclosed himself
in a room with two bottles of gin, later
fell the length of his body
so that brain blood moved
to new compartments
that never knew the wash of fluid
and he died in minutes of a new equilibrium.

His early life was a terrifying comedy
and my mother divorced him again and again.
He would rush into tunnels magnetized
by the white eye of trains
and once, gaining instant fame,
managed to stop a Perahara in Ceylon
 – the whole procession of elephants dancers
local dignitaries – by falling
dead drunk onto the street.

As a semi-official, and semi-white at that,
the act was seen as a crucial
turning point in the Home Rule Movement
and led to Ceylon's independence in 1948.

(My mother had done her share too—
her driving so bad
she was stoned by villagers
whenever her car was recognized)

For 14 years of marriage
each of them claimed he or she
was the injured party.
Once on the Colombo docks
saying goodbye to a recently married couple
my father, jealous
at my mother's articulate emotion,
dove into the waters of the harbour
and swam after the ship waving farewell.
My mother pretending no affiliation
mingled with the crowd back to the hotel.

Once again he made the papers
though this time my mother
with a note to the editor
corrected the report – saying he was drunk
rather than broken hearted at the parting of friends.
The married couple received both editions
of *The Ceylon Times* when their ship reached Aden.

And then in his last years
he was the silent drinker,
the man who once a week
disappeared into his room with bottles
and stayed there until he was drunk
and until he was sober.

There speeches, head dreams, apologies,

the gentle letters, were composed.
With the clarity of architects
he would write of the row of blue flowers
his new wife had planted,
the plans for electricity in the house,
how my half-sister fell near a snake
and it had awakened and not touched her.
Letters in a clear hand of the most complete empathy
his heart widening and widening and widening
to all manner of change in his children and friends
while he himself edged
into the terrible acute hatred
of his own privacy
till he balanced and fell
the length of his body
the blood entering
the empty reservoir of bones
the blood searching in his head without metaphor.

GRIFFIN OF THE NIGHT

I'm holding my son in my arms
sweating after nightmares
small me
fingers in his mouth
his other fist clenched in my hair
small me
sweating after nightmares.

BIRTH OF SOUND

At night the most private of a dog's long body groan.
It comes with his last stretch
in the dark corridor outside our room.
The children turn.
A window tries to split with cold
the other dog hoofing the carpet for lice.
We're all alone.

WE'RE AT THE GRAVEYARD

Stuart Sally Kim and I
watching still stars
or now and then sliding stars
like hawk spit to the trees.
Up there the clear charts,
the systems' intricate branches
which change with hours and solstices,
the bone geometry of moving from there, to there.

And down here – friends
whose minds and bodies
shift like acrobats to each other.
When we leave, they move
to an altitude of silence.

So our minds shape
and lock the transient,
parallel these bats
who organize the air
with thick blinks of travel.
Sally is like grey snow in the grass.
Sally of the beautiful bones
pregnant below stars.

NEAR ELGINBURG

3 a.m. on the floor mattress.
In my pyjamas a moth beats frantic
my heart is breaking loose.

I have been dreaming of a man
who places honey on his forehead before sleep
so insects come tempted by liquid
to sip past it into the brain.
In the morning his head contains wings
and the soft skeletons of wasp.

Our suicide into nature.
That man's seduction
so he can beat the itch
against the floor and give in
move among the sad remnants
of those we have destroyed,
the torn code these animals ride to death on.
Grey fly on windowsill
white fish by the dock
heaved like a slimy bottle into the deep,
to end up as snake
heckled by children and cameras
as he crosses lawns of civilization.

We lie on the floor mattress
lost moths walk on us
waterhole of flesh, want
this humiliation under the moon.
Till in the morning we are surrounded
by dark virtuous ships
sent by the kingdom of the loon.

LOOP

My last dog poem.
I leave behind all social animals
including my dog who takes
30 seconds dismounting from a chair.
Turn to the one
who appears again on roads
one eye torn out and chasing.

He is only a space filled
and blurred with passing,
transient as shit – will fade
to reappear somewhere else.

He survives the porcupine, cars, poison,
fences with their spasms of electricity.
Vomits up bones, bathes at night
in Holiday Inn swimming pools.

And magic in his act of loss.
The missing eye travels up
in a bird's mouth, and into the sky.
Departing family. It is loss only of flesh
no more than his hot spurt across a tree.

He is the one you see at Drive-Ins
tearing silent into garbage
while societies unfold in his sky.
The bird lopes into the rectangle nest of images

and parts of him move on.

HERON REX

Mad kings
blood lines introverted, strained pure
so the brain runs in the wrong direction

they are proud of their heritage of suicides
– not just the ones who went mad
balancing on that goddamn leg, but those

whose eyes turned off
the sun and imagined it
those who looked north, those who
forced their feathers to grow in
those who couldn't find the muscles in their arms
who drilled their beaks into the skin
those who could speak
and lost themselves in the foul connections
who crashed against black bars in a dream of escape
those who moved round the dials of imaginary clocks
those who fell asleep and never woke
who never slept and so dropped dead
those who attacked the casual eyes of children and were led away
and those who faced corners for ever
those who exposed themselves and were led away
those who pretended broken limbs, epilepsy,
who managed to electrocute themselves on wire
those who felt their skin was on fire and screamed
                         and were led away

There are ways of going
physically mad, physically
mad when you perfect the mind
where you sacrifice yourself for the race
when you are the representative when you allow
yourself to be paraded in the cages
celebrity a razor in the body

These small birds so precise
frail as morning neon
they are royalty melted down
they are the glass core at the heart of kings
yet 15-year-old boys could enter the cage
and break them in minutes
as easily as a long fingernail

RAT JELLY

See the rat in the jelly
steaming dirty hair
frozen, bring it out on a glass tray
split the pie four ways and eat
I took great care cooking this treat for you
and tho it looks good
and tho it smells of the Westinghouse still
and tastes of exotic fish or
maybe the expensive arse of a cow
I want you to know it's rat
steaming dirty hair and still alive

(caught him last Sunday
thinking of the fridge, thinking of you.)

KING KONG MEETS WALLACE STEVENS

Take two photographs—
Wallace Stevens and King Kong
(Is it significant that I eat bananas as I write this?)

Stevens is portly, benign, a white brush cut
striped tie. Businessman but
for the dark thick hands, the naked brain
the thought in him.

Kong is staggering
lost in New York streets again
a spawn of annoyed cars at his toes.
The mind is nowhere.
Fingers are plastic, electric under the skin.
He's at the call of Metro-Goldwyn-Mayer.

Meanwhile W. S. in his suit
is thinking chaos is thinking fences.
In his head – the seeds of fresh pain
his exorcising,
the bellow of locked blood.

The hands drain from his jacket,
pose in the murderer's shadow.

'THE GATE IN HIS HEAD'

for Victor Coleman

Victor, the shy mind
revealing the faint scars
coloured strata of the brain,
not clarity but the sense of shift

a few lines, the tracks of thought

Landscape of busted trees
the melted tires in the sun
Stan's fishbowl
with a book inside
turning its pages
like some sea animal
camouflaging itself
the typeface clarity
going slow blonde in the sun full water

My mind is pouring chaos
in nets onto the page.
A blind lover, dont know
what I love till I write it out.
And then from Gibson's your letter
with a blurred photograph of a gull.
Caught vision. The stunning white bird
an unclear stir.

And that is all this writing should be then.
The beautiful formed things caught at the wrong moment
so they are shapeless, awkward
moving to the clear.

TAKING

It is the formal need
to suck blossoms out of the flesh
in those we admire
planting them private in the brain
and cause fruit in lonely gardens.

To learn to pour the exact arc
of steel still soft and crazy
before it hits the page.
I have stroked the mood and tone
of hundred year dead men and women
Emily Dickinson's large dog, Conrad's beard
and, for myself,
removed them from historical traffic.
Having tasted their brain. Or heard
the wet sound of a death cough.
Their idea of the immaculate moment is now.

The rumours pass on
the rumours pass on
are planted
till they become a spine.

BURNING HILLS

for Kris and Fred

So he came to write again
in the burnt hill region
north of Kingston. A cabin
with mildew spreading down walls.
Bullfrogs on either side of him.

Hanging his lantern of Shell Vapona Strip
on a hook in the centre of the room
he waited a long time. Opened
the Hilroy writing pad, yellow Bic pen.
Every summer he believed would be his last.
This schizophrenic season change, June to September,
when he deviously thought out plots
across the character of his friends.
Sometimes barren as fear going nowhere
or in habit meaningless as tapwater.
One year maybe he would come and sit
for four months and not write a word down
would sit and investigate colours, the
insects in the room with him.

What he brought: a typewriter
tins of ginger ale, cigarettes. A copy of *Strangelove*,
of *The Intervals*, a postcard of Rousseau's *The Dream*.
His friends' words were strict as lightning
unclothing the bark of a tree, a shaved hook.
The postcard was a test pattern by the window
through which he saw growing scenery.

Eventually the room was a time machine for him.
He closed the rotting door, sat down
thought pieces of history. The first girl
who in a park near his school
put a warm hand into his trousers
unbuttoning and finally catching the spill
across her wrist, he in the maze of her skirt.
She later played the piano
when he had tea with the parents.
He remembered that surprised—
he had forgotten for so long.
Under raincoats in the park on hot days.

The summers were layers of civilization in his memory
they were old photographs he didn't look at anymore
for girls in them were chubby not as perfect as in his mind
and his ungovernable hair was shaved to the edge of skin.
His friends leaned on bicycles
were 16 and tried to look 21
the cigarettes too big for their faces.
He could read those characters easily
undisguised as wedding pictures.
He could hardly remember their names
though they had talked all day, exchanged styles
and like dogs on a lawn hung around the houses of girls.

Sex a game of targets, of throwing firecrackers
at a couple in a field locked in hand-made orgasms,
singing dramatically in someone's ear along with the record
'How do you think I feel / you know our love's not real
The one you're made about / Is just a gad-about
How do you think I feel'.
He saw all that complex tension the way his children would.

There is one picture that fuses the five summers.
Eight of them are leaning against a wall
arms around each other
looking into the camera and the sun
trying to smile at the unseen adult photographer
trying against the glare to look 21 and confident.
The summer and friendship will last forever.
Except one who was eating an apple. That was him
oblivious to the significance of the moment.
Now he hungers to have that arm around the next shoulder.
The wretched apple is fresh and white.

Since he began burning hills
the Shell strip has taken effect.
A wasp is crawling on the floor
tumbling over, its motor fanatic.
He has smoked 5 cigarettes.
He has written slowly and carefully
with great love and great coldness.
When he finishes he will go back
hunting for the lies that are obvious.

CHARLES DARWIN PAYS A VISIT,
DECEMBER 1971

View of the coast of Brazil.
A man stood up to shout
at the image of a sailing ship
which was a vast white bird from over the sea
now ripping its claws into the ocean.
Faded hills of March
painted during the cold morning.
On board ship Charles Darwin sketched clouds.

One of these days the Prime Mover will
paint the Prime Mover out of his sky.
I want a . . . centuries being displaced
   . . . faith

                23rd of June, 1832.
                He caught sixty-eight species
                of a particularly minute beetle.

The blue thick leaves who greeted him
animals unconscious of celebration
moved slowly into law.
Adam with a watch.
Look past and future, (*I want a . . .*),
ease our way out of the structures
this smell of the cogs
and diamonds we live in.

I am waiting for a new ship, so new
we will think the lush machine
an animal of God.
Weary from travelling over the air and the water
it will sink to its feet at our door.

THE VAULT

Having to put forward candidates for God
I nominate Henri Rousseau and Dr Bucke,
tired of the lizard paradise
whose image banks renew off the flesh of others
– those stories that hate, which are remnants and insults.
Refresh where plants breed to the edge of dream.

I have woken to find myself covered in white sheets
walls and doors, food.
There was no food in the world I left
where I ate the rich air. The bodies of small birds
who died while flying fell into my mouth.
Fruit dripped through our thirst to the earth.

All night the traffic of apes floats across the sky
a worm walks through the gaze of a lion
some birds live all their evenings on one branch.

They are held by the celebration of God's wife.
In Rousseau's *The Dream* she is the naked lady
who has been animal and tree
her breast a suckled orange.
The fibres and fluids of their moral nature
have seeped within her frame.

The hand is outstretched
her fingers move out in
mutual transfusion to the place.
Our low speaking last night
was barely audible among the grunt
of mongrel meditation.

She looks to the left
for that is the direction we leave in
when we fall from her room of flowers.

WHITE DWARFS

This is for people who disappear
for those who descend into the code
and make their room a fridge for Superman
— who exhaust costume and bones that could perform flight,
who shave their moral so raw
they can tear themselves through the eye of a needle
this is for those people
that hover and hover
and die in the ether peripheries

There is my fear
of no words   of
falling without words
over and over   of
mouthing the silence
Why do I love most
among my heroes those
who sail to that perfect edge
where there is no social fuel
Release of sandbags
to understand their altitude—

              that silence of the third cross
              3rd man hung so high and lonely
              we don't hear him say
              say his pain, say his unbrotherhood
              What has he to do with the smell of ladies,
              can they eat off his skeleton of pain?

The Gurkhas in Malaya
cut the tongues of mules
so they were silent beasts of burden
in enemy territories
after such cruelty what could they speak of anyway
And Dashiell Hammett in success

suffered conversation and moved
to the perfect white between the words

This white that can grow
is fridge, bed,
is an egg – most beautiful
when unbroken, where
what we cannot see is growing
in all the colours we cannot see

there are those burned out stars
who implode into silence
after parading in the sky
after such choreography what would they wish to speak of   anyway

'Newly arrived and totally ignorant of the Levantine languages, Marco Polo could express himself only with gestures, leaps, cries of wonder and of horror, animal barkings or hootings, or with objects he took from his knapsacks – ostrich plumes, pea-shooters, quartzes – which he arranged in front of him . . . '

ITALO CALVINO

THE AGATHA CHRISTIE BOOKS
BY THE WINDOW

In the long open Vancouver Island room
sitting by the indoor avocados
where indoor spring light
falls on the half covered bulbs

and down the long room light falling
onto the dwarf orange tree
vines from south america
the agatha christie books by the window

Nameless morning
solution of grain and colour

There is this light,
colourless, which falls on the warm
stretching brain of the bulb
that is dreaming avocado

COUNTRY NIGHT

The bathroom light burns over the mirror

In the blackness of the house
beds groan from the day's exhaustion
hold the tired shoulders bruised
and cut legs the unexpected
3 a.m. erections. Someone's dream
involves a saw someone's
dream involves a woman.
We have all dreamed of finding the lost dog.

The last light on upstairs
throws a circular pattern
through the decorated iron vent
to become a living room's moon.

The sofa calls the dog, the cat
in perfect blackness walks over the stove.
In the room of permanent light
cockroaches march on enamel.
The spider with jewel coloured thighs the brown moth
with corporal stripes
                              ascend pipes
and look into mirrors.

All night the truth happens.

MOVING FRED'S OUTHOUSE/
GERIATRICS OF PINE

All afternoon (while the empty drive-in
screen in the distance promises)
we are moving the two-seater
100 yards across his garden

We turn it over on its top
and over, and as it slowly
falls on its side
the children cheer

60 years old and a change in career—
from these pale yellow flowers emerging
out of damp wood in the roof
to become a room thorough with flight, noise,
and pregnant with the morning's eggs,
a perch for chickens.

Two of us. The sweat.
Our hands under the bottom
then the top as it goes
over, through twin holes the
flowers, running to move the roller, shove,
and everybody screaming to keep the dog away.
Fred the pragmatist – dragging the ancient comic
out of retirement and into a television series
among the charging democracy of rhode island reds

Head over heels across the back lawn
old wood collapsing in our hands

All afternoon the silent space is turned

BUCK LAKE STORE AUCTION

Scrub lawn.
        A chained
dog tense and smelling.
50 cents for a mattress. 50 cents
for doors that allowed privacy.

              A rain
swollen copy of Jack London
a magazine drawing of a rabbit
bordered with finishing nails.
6 chickens, bird cage (empty),
sauerkraut cutting board

down to the rock
          trees

not bothering to look
into the old woman's eyes
as we go in, get a number
have the power to bid
on everything that is exposed.
After an hour in this sun
I expected her to unscrew
her left arm and donate it
to the auctioneer's excitement.
In certain rituals we desire
only what we cannot have.
While for her, Mrs Germain,
this is the needle's eye
where maniacs of earth select.
Look, I wanted to say,
$10 for the dog
with faded denim eyes

FARRE OFF

There are the poems of Campion I never saw till now
and Wyatt who loved with the best
and suddenly I want 16th-century women
round me devious politic aware
of step ladders to the king

Tonight I am alone with dogs and lightning
aroused by Wyatt's talk of women who step
naked into his bedchamber

Moonlight and barnlight constant
lightning every second minute
I have on my thin blue parka
and walk behind the asses of the dogs
who slide under the gate
and sense cattle
deep in the fields

I look out into the dark pasture
past where even the moonlight stops

my eyes are against the ink of Campion

WALKING TO BELLROCK

Two figures in deep water.

Their frames truncated at the stomach
glide along the surface. Depot Creek.
One hundred years ago lumber being driven down this river
tore and shovelled and widened the banks into Bellrock
down past bridges to the mill.

The two figures are walking
as if half sunk in a grey road
their feet tentative, stumbling on stone bottom.
Landscapes underwater. What do the feet miss?
Turtle, watersnake, clam. What do the feet ignore
and the brain not look at, as two figures slide
past George Grant's green immaculate fields
past the splashed blood of cardinal flower on the bank.

Rivers are a place for philosophy but all thought
is about the mechanics of this river is about
stones that twist your ankles
the hidden rocks you walk your knee into—
feet in slow motion and brain and balanced arms
imagining the blind path of foot, underwater sun
suddenly catching the almond coloured legs
the torn old Adidas tennis shoes we wear
to walk the river into Bellrock.

What is the conversation about for three hours
on this winding twisted evasive river to town?
What was the conversation about all summer.
Stan and I laughing joking going summer crazy
as we lived against each other.
To keep warm we submerge. Sometimes
just our heads decapitated
glide on the dark glass.

There is no metaphor here.
We are aware of the heat of the water, coldness of the rain,
smell of mud in certain sections that farts
when you step on it, mud never walked on
so you can't breathe, my god you can't breathe this air
and you swim fast your feet off the silt of history
that was there when the logs went
leaping down for the Rathburn Timber Company
when those who stole logs had to leap
right out of the country if caught.

But there is no history or philosophy or metaphor with us.
The problem is the toughness of the Adidas shoe
its three stripes gleaming like fish decoration.
The story is Russell's arm waving out of the green of a field.

The plot of the afternoon is to get to Bellrock
through rapids, falls, stink water
and reach the island where beer and a towel wait for us.
That night there is not even pain in our newly used muscles
not even the puckering of flesh
and little to tell except you won't
believe how that river winds and when you
don't see the feet you concentrate on the feet.
And all the next day trying to think
what we didn't talk about.
Where was the criminal conversation
broken sentences lost in the splash in wind.

Stan, my crazy summer friend,
why are we both going crazy?
Going down to Bellrock
recognizing home by the colour of barns
which tell us north, south, west,
and otherwise lost in miles and miles of rain
in the middle of this century
following the easy fucking stupid plot to town.

PIG GLASS

Bonjour.   This is pig glass
a piece of cloudy sea

nosed out of the earth by swine
and smoothed into pebble
run it across your cheek
it will not cut you

and this is my hand a language
which was buried for years   touch it
against your stomach

                    The pig glass
I thought
was the buried eye of Portland Township
slow faded history
waiting to be grunted up
There is no past until you breathe
on such green glass
                    rub it
over your stomach and cheek

The Meeks family used this section
years ago to bury tin
crockery forks dog tags
and each morning
pigs ease up that ocean
redeeming it again
into the possibilities of rust
one morning I found a whole axle
another day a hand crank
but this is pig glass
tested with narrow teeth
and let lie. The morning's green present.
Portland Township jewellery.

There is the band from the ankle of a pigeon
a weathered bill from the Bellrock Cheese Factory
letters in 1925 to a dead mother I
disturbed in the room above the tractor shed.
Journals of family love
servitude to farm weather
a work glove in a cardboard box
creased flat and hard like a flower.

A bottle thrown   .
by loggers out of a wagon
past midnight
explodes against rock.
This green fragment has behind it
the *booomm* when glass
tears free of its smoothness

now once more smooth as knuckle
a tooth on my tongue.
Comfort that bites through skin
hides in the dark afternoon of my pocket.
Snake shade.
Determined histories of glass.

THE HOUR OF COWDUST

It is the hour we move small
in the last possibilities of light

now the sky opens its blue vault

I thought this hour belonged to my children
bringing cows home
bored by duty swinging a stick,
but this focus of dusk out of dust
is everywhere – here by the Nile
the boats wheeling
like massive half-drowned birds
and I gaze at water that dreams
dust off my tongue,
in this country your mouth
feels the way your shoes look

Everything is reducing itself to shape

Lack of light cools your shirt
men step from barbershops
their skin alive to the air.
All day
dust covered granite hills
and now
suddenly the Nile is flesh
an arm on a bed

In Indian miniatures
I cannot quite remember
what this hour means
– people were small,
animals represented
simply by dust
they stamped into the air.
All I recall of commentaries
are abrupt lovely sentences where
the colour of a bowl
a left foot stepping on a lotus
symbolized separation.
Or stories of gods
creating such beautiful women
they themselves burned in passion
and were reduced to ash.
Women confided to pet parrots
solitary men dreamed into the conch.
So many
graciously humiliated
by the distance of rivers

The boat turns languid
under the hunched passenger
sails
ready for the moon
fill like a lung

there is no longer
depth of perception
it is now possible
for the outline of two boats
to collide silently

THE PALACE

7 a.m.   The hour of red daylight

I walk through palace grounds
waking the sentries
                    scarves
around their neck and mouths
leak breath mist
The gibbons stroll
twenty feet high
through turret arches
and on the edge
of brown parapet
I am alone
            leaning
            into flying air

Ancient howls of a king
who released his aviary
like a wave to the city below
celebrating the day of his birth
and they when fed
would return to his hand
like the payment of grain

All over Rajasthan
palaces die young
                    at this height
                    a red wind
my shirt and sweater cold

From the white city below
a beautiful wail
of a woman's voice rises
300 street transistors
simultaneously playing
the one radio station of Udaipur

USWETAKEIYAWA

Uswetakeiyawa. The night mile

through the village of tall
thorn leaf fences
sudden odours
which pour through windows of the jeep.

We see nothing, just
the grey silver of the Dutch canal
where bright coloured boats
lap like masks in the night
their alphabets lost in the dark.

No sight but the imagination's
story behind each smell
or now and then a white sarong
pumping its legs on a bicycle
like a moth in the headlights

       and the dogs
who lean out of night
strolling the road
with eyes of sapphire
and hideous body
           so mongrelled
they seem to have woken
to find themselves tricked
into outrageous transformations,
one with the spine of a snake
one with a creature in its mouth
(car lights rouse them
from the purity of darkness).

This is the dream journey
we travel most nights
returning from Colombo.

The road hugs the canal
the canal every mile
puts an arm into the sea.

In daylight women bathe
waist deep beside the road
utterly still as I drive past
their diya reddha cloth
tied under their arms.
Brief sentences of women
lean men with soapy buttocks
their arms stretching up
to pour water over themselves,
or the ancient man in spectacles
crossing the canal
only his head visible
pulling something we cannot see
in the water behind him.
The women surface
bodies the colour of shadow
wet bright cloth
the skin of a mermaid.

In the silence of the night drive
you hear ocean you swallow odours
which change each minute – dried fish
swamp toddy a variety of curries
and something we have never been able to recognize.
There is just this thick air
and the aura of dogs
in trickster skin.

Once in the night we saw
something slip into the canal.
There was then the odour we did not recognize.
The smell of a dog losing its shape.

THE WARS

Dusk in Colombo

the Bo tree   dark all day
gathers the last of our light

and in its green rooms which yawn
over Pettah stores
is its own shadow
– hundreds of unseen bats
tuning up the auditorium
in archaic Tamil

Trincomalee
                    they whisper
is my brother
source of my exile
long slow miles to the scrub north
whose blossoms are dirty birds
so bright they are extracts of the sea

Swim
      into the north's blue eye
over the milk floor of ocean
that darkens only with depth

The Ray
flies in silence
muttering bubbles to himself
Tread over his avenue

The ancient warrior
whose brother
stole his operatic tongue

                    plunges

in pure muscle
towards his neighbours
bloodless   full
of noon moonlight

only his twin
knows how to charm
the waters against him

SWEET LIKE A CROW

for Hetti Corea, 8 years old

*'The Sinhalese are beyond a doubt one of the least musical
people in the world. It would be quite impossible to have
less sense of pitch, line or rhythm'* PAUL BOWLES

Your voice sounds like a scorpion being pushed
through a glass tube
like someone has just trod on a peacock
like wind howling in a coconut
like a rusty bible, like someone pulling barbed wire
across a stone courtyard, like a pig drowning,
a vattacka being fried
a bone shaking hands
a frog singing at Carnegie Hall.

Like a crow swimming in milk,
like a nose being hit by a mango
like the crowd at the Royal-Thomian match,
a womb full of twins, a pariah dog
with a magpie in its mouth
like the midnight jet from Casablanca
like Air Pakistan curry,
a typewriter on fire, like a hundred
pappadans being crunched, like someone
trying to light matches in a dark room,
the clicking sound of a reef when you put your head into the sea,
a dolphin reciting epic poetry to a sleepy audience,
the sound of a fan when someone throws brinjals at it,
like pineapples being sliced in the Pettah market
like betel juice hitting a butterfly in mid-air
like a whole village running naked onto the street
and tearing their sarongs, like an angry family
pushing a jeep out of the mud, like dirt on the needle,
like 8 sharks being carried on the back of a bicycle
like 3 old ladies locked in the lavatory
like the sound I heard when having an afternoon sleep
and someone walked through my room in ankle bracelets.

67

LATE MOVIES WITH SKYLER

All week since he's been home
he has watched late movies alone
terrible one star films and then staggering
through the dark house to his bed
waking at noon to work on the broken car
he has come home to fix.

21 years old and restless
back from logging on Vancouver Island
with men who get rid of crabs with Raid
    2 minutes bending over in agony
    and then into the showers!

Last night I joined him for *The Prisoner of Zenda*
a film I saw three times in my youth
and which no doubt influenced me morally.
Hot coffee bananas and cheese
we are ready at 11.30 for adventure.

At each commercial Sky
breaks into midnight guitar practice
head down playing loud and intensely
till the movie comes on and the music suddenly stops.
Skyler's favourite hours when he's usually alone
cooking huge meals of anything in the frying pan
thumbing through *Advanced Guitar* like a bible.
We talk during the film
and break into privacy during commercials
or get more coffee or push
the screen door open and urinate under the trees.

Laughing at the dilemmas of 1920 heroes
suggestive lines, cutaways to court officials
who raise their eyebrows at least 4 inches
when the lovers kiss . . .
only the anarchy of the evil Rupert of Hentzau
is appreciated.
                    And still somehow
by 1.30 we are moved
as Stewart Granger girl-less and countryless
rides into the sunset with his morals and his horse.
The perfect world is over. Banana peels
orange peels ashtrays guitar books.
2 a.m. We stagger through
into the slow black rooms of the house.

I lie in bed fully awake. The darkness
breathes to the pace of a dog's snoring.
The film is replayed to sounds
of an intricate blues guitar.
Skyler is Rupert then the hero.
He will leave in a couple of days
for Montreal or the Maritimes.
In the movies of my childhood the heroes
after skilled swordplay and moral victories
leave with absolutely nothing
to do for the rest of their lives.

SALLIE CHISUM/LAST WORDS
ON BILLY THE KID 4 A.M.

for Nancy Beatty

The moon hard and yellow where Billy's head is.
I have been moving in my room
these last 5 minutes. Looking for a cigarette.
That is a sin he taught me.
Showed me how to hold it and how to want it.

I had been looking and stepped forward
to feel along the windowsill
and there was the tanned moon head.
His body the shadow of the only tree on the property.

I am at the table.
Billy's mouth is trying
to remove a splinter out of my foot.
Tough skin on the bottom of me.
Still. I can feel his teeth
bite precise. And then moving his face back
holding something in his grin, says he's got it.

Where have you been I ask
Where have you been he replies

I have been into every room about 300 times
since you were here
I have walked about 60 miles in this house
Where have you been I ask

Billy was a fool
he was like those reversible mirrors
you can pivot round and see youself again
but there is something showing on the other side always.
Sunlight. The shade beside the cupboard.

He fired two bullets into the dummy
on which I built dresses
where the nipples should have been.
That wasn't too funny, but we laughed a lot.

One morning he was still sleeping
I pushed the door and watched him from the hall
he looked like he was having a serious dream.
Concentrating. Angry. As if wallpaper
had been ripped off a wall.

Billy's mouth at my foot
removing the splinter.
Did I say that?

It was just before lunch one day.

I have been alive
37 years since I knew him. He was a fool.
He was like those mirrors I told you about.

I am leaning against the bed rail
I have finished my cigarette
now I cannnot find the ashtray.
I put it out, squash it
against the window
where the moon is.
In his stupid eyes.

PURE MEMORY/CHRIS DEWDNEY

'Listen, it was so savage and brutal and powerful
that even though it happened out of the blue I
knew there was nothing arbitrary about it'

CHRISTOPHER DEWDNEY

I

On a B.C. radio show the man asked me, coffee half way up to
his mouth, what are the books you've liked recently? Christopher
Dewdney's *A Palaeozoic Geology of London Ontario*. Only I didn't say
that, I started stumbling on the word Palaeozoic . . . Paleo . . .
Polio . . . and then it happened on Geology too until it seemed a
disease. I sounded like an idiot. Meanwhile I was watching the
man's silent gulps. The professional silent gulping of coffee an
inch or two away from the microphone. Unconcerned with my
sinking 'live' all over the province.

2

I can't remember where I first met him. Somewhere I became
aware of this giggle. Tan hair, tan face, tan shirt and a giggle-
snort as his head staggered back. His arms somewhere.

3

The baby. He shows me the revolving globe in the 4-month-old
kid's crib. Only it has been unscrewed and the globe turned
upside down and rescrewed in that way so Africa and Asia all
swivel upside down. This way he says she'll have to come to
terms with the shapes all over again when she grows up.

4

He comes to dinner, steps out of the car and transforms the
10-year-old suburban garden into ancient history. Is on his knees
pointing out the age and race and character of rocks and earth.
He loves the Norfolk Pine. I give him a piece of wood 120 million
years old from the tar sands and he smokes a bit of it.

5

When he was a kid and his parents had guests and he was
eventually told to get to bed he liked to embarrass them by
running under a table and screaming out Don't hit me
Don't hit me.

6

His most embarrassing moment. A poetry reading in Toronto.
He was sitting in the front row and he realized that he hated the
poetry. He looked around discreetly for the exit but it was a long
way away. Then to the right, quite near him, he saw another door.
As a poem ended he got up and officially walked to the door
quickly opened it went out and closed it behind him. He found
himself in a dark cupboard about 2 feet by 3 feet. It contained
nothing. He waited there for a while, then he started to laugh and
giggle. He giggled for 5 minutes and he thinks the audience could
probably hear him. When he had collected himself he opened the
door, came out, walked to his seat and sat down again.

7

Coach House Press, December 1974. I haven't seen him for a
long time. His face is tough. Something has left his face. It is
not that he is thinner but the face has lost something distinct
and it seems like flesh. But he is not thinner. He is busy
working on his new book *Fovea Centralis* and I watch him as he

sits in the empty back room upstairs all alone with a computer typesetting terminal. I can't get over his face. It is 'tight', as if a stocking were over it and he about to perform a robbery. He plucks at the keys and talks down into the machine. I am relieved when he starts giggling at something. I tell him I'm coming down to London in a week and he says he will show me his butterflies, he has bought two mounted butterflies for a very good price. If I don't tell anyone he will let me know where I could get one. A Chinaman in London Ontario sells them. I start to laugh. He doesn't. This is serious information, important rare information like the history of rocks – these frail wings of almost powder have their genealogies too.

8

His favourite movie is *Earthquake*. He stands in the middle of his apartment very excited telling me all the details. He shows me his beautiful fossils, a small poster of James Dean hitting his brother in *East of Eden*, and the two very impressive mounted butterflies.

9

On the bus going back to Toronto I have a drawing of him by Robert Fones. Wrapped in brown paper it lies above me on the luggage rack. When the bus swerves I put my arm out into the dark aisle ready to catch him if it falls. A strange drawing of him in his cane chair with a plant to the side of him, reading Frank O'Hara with very oriental eyes. It was done in 1973, before the flesh left his face.

10

His wife's brain haemorrhage. I could not cope with that. He is 23 years old. He does. Africa Asia Australia upside down. Earthquake.

BEARHUG

Griffin calls to come and kiss him goodnight
I yell ok. Finish something I'm doing,
then something else, walk slowly round
the corner to my son's room.
He is standing arms outstretched
waiting for a bearhug. Grinning.

Why do I give my emotion an animal's name,
give it that dark squeeze of death?
This is the hug which collects
all his small bones and his warm neck against me.
The thin tough body under the pyjamas
locks to me like a magnet of blood.

How long was he standing there
like that, before I came?

Elimination Dance
(an intermission)

'Nothing I'd read prepared me for a body this unfair'

JOHN NEWLOVE

'Till we be roten, kan we not be rypen'

GEOFFREY CHAUCER

Those who are allergic to the sea

Those who have resisted depravity

Men who shave off beards in stages, pausing to take photographs

American rock stars who wear Toronto Maple Leaf hockey sweaters

Those who (while visiting a foreign country) have lost the end of a Q tip in their ear and have been unable to explain their problem

Gentlemen who have placed a microphone beside a naked woman's stomach after lunch and later, after slowing down the sound considerably, have sold these noises on the open market as whale songs

All actors and poets who spit into the first row while they perform

Men who fear to use an electric lawn-mower feeling they could drowse off and be dragged by it into a swimming pool

Any dinner guest who has consumed the host's missing contact lens along with the dessert

Any person who has had the following dream. You are in a subway station of a major city. At the far end you see a coffee machine. You put in two coins. The Holy Grail drops down. Then blood pours into the chalice

Any person who has lost a urine sample in the mail

All those belle-lettrists who feel that should have been '*an* urine sample'

Anyone who has had to step into an elevator with all of the Irish Rovers

Those who have filled in a bilingual and confidential pig survey from Statistics Canada. (Une enquête sur les porcs, strictement confidentielle)

Those who have written to the age old brotherhood of Rosicrucians for a free copy of their book 'The Mastery of Life' in order to release the inner consciousness and to experience (in the privacy of the home) momentary flights of the soul

Those who have accidently stapled themselves

Anyone who has been penetrated by a mountie

Any university professor who has danced with a life-sized cardboard cut-out of Jean Genet

Those who have unintentionally locked themselves within a sleeping bag at a camping goods store

Any woman whose i.u.d. has set off an alarm system at the airport

Those who, after a swim, find the sensation of water dribbling out of their ears erotic

Men who have never touched a whippet

Women who gave up the accordion because of pinched breasts

Those who have pissed out of the back of moving trucks

Those who have woken to find the wet footprints of a peacock across their kitchen floor

Anyone whose knees have been ruined as a result of performing sexual acts in elevators

Those who have so much as contemplated the possibility of creeping up to one's enemy with two Bic lighters, pressing simultaneously the butane switches – one into each nostril – and so gassing him to death

Literary critics who have swum the Hellespont

Anyone who has been hired as a 'professional beater' and frightened grouse in the direction of the Queen Mother

Any lover who has gone into a flower shop on Valentine's Day and asked for clitoris when he meant clematis

Those who have come across their own telephone numbers underneath terse insults or compliments in the washroom of the Bay Street Bus Terminal

Those who have used the following techniques of seduction:
-small talk at a falconry convention
-entering a spa town disguised as Ford Madox Ford
-making erotic rotations of the pelvis, backstage, during the storm scene of *King Lear*
-underlining suggestive phrases in the prefaces of Joseph Conrad

Anyone who has testified as a character witness for a dog in a court of law

Any writer who has been photographed for the jacket of a book in one of the following poses: sitting in the back of a 1956 Dodge with two roosters; in a tuxedo with the Sydney Opera House in the distance; studying the vanishing point on a jar of Dutch Cleanser; against a gravestone with dramatic back lighting; with a false nose on; in the vicinity of Macchu Pichu; or sitting in a study and looking intensely at one's own book

The person who borrowed my Martin Beck thriller, read it in
a sauna which melted the glue off the spine so the pages drifted
to the floor, stapled them together and returned the book,
thinking I wouldn't notice

Any person who has burst into tears at the Liquor Control
Board

Anyone with pain

Secular Love

'You're an actor, aren't you?'

The man nodded silently and averted his eyes.

'I've seen you in films. You always seem embarrassed at the thought of what you have to say next.'

The man laughed and again averted his eyes.

'Your trouble, I believe, is that you always hold back something of yourself. You're not shameless enough for an actor. In my opinion you should learn how to run properly and scream properly, with your mouth wide open. I've noticed that even when you yawn you're afraid to open your mouth all the way. In your next film make a sign to show that you've understood me. You haven't even been discovered yet. I'm looking forward to seeing you grow older from film to film.'

PETER HANDKE The left-handed woman

Claude Glass

A somewhat convex dark or coloured hand-mirror, used to concentrate the features of the landscape in subdued tones.
   'Grey walked about everywhere with that pretty toy, the claude glass, in his hand, making the beautiful forms of the landscape compose in its luscious chiaroscuro.' Gosse (1882)

He is told about
the previous evening's behaviour.

Starting with a punchbowl
on the volleyball court.
Dancing and falling across coffee tables,
asking his son Are *you* the bastard
who keeps telling me I'm drunk?
kissing the limbs of women
suspicious of his friends serenading
five pigs by the barn
heaving a wine glass towards garden
and continually going through gates
into the dark fields
and collapsing.
His wife half carrying him home
rescuing him from departing cars,
complains this morning
of a sore shoulder.
                    And even later
his thirteen-year-old daughter's struggle
to lift him into the back kitchen
after he has passed out, resting his head on rocks,
wondering what he was looking for in dark fields.

For he has always loved that ancient darkness
where the flat rocks glide like Japanese tables
where he can remove clothes
and lie with moonlight on the day's heat
hardened in stone, drowning
in this star blanket this sky
like a giant trout

conscious how the heaven
careens over him
as he moves in back fields
kissing the limbs of trees
or placing ear on stone which rocks him
and then stands to watch the house
in its oasis of light.
And he knows something is happening there to him
solitary while he spreads his arms
and holds everything that is slipping away together.

He is suddenly in the heat of the party
slouching towards women, revolving
round one unhappy shadow.
That friend who said he would find
the darkest place, and then wave.
He is not a lost drunk
like his father or his friend, can,
he says, stop on a dime, and he can
he could because even now, now in
this brilliant darkness where
grass has lost its colour and it's all
fucking Yeats and moonlight, he knows
this colourless grass is making his bare feet green
for it is the hour of magic
which no matter what sadness
leaves him grinning.
At certain hours of the night
ducks are nothing but landscape
just voices breaking as they nightmare.
The weasel wears their blood
home like a scarf,
cows drain over the horizon
                              and the dark
vegetables hum onward underground

but the mouth
        wants plum.

Moves from room to room
where brown beer glass
smashed lounges at his feet
opens the long rust stained gate
and steps towards invisible fields
that he knows from years of daylight.
He snorts in the breeze
which carries a smell
of cattle on its back.

What this place does not have
is the white paint of bathing cabins
the leak of eucalyptus.
During a full moon
outcrops of rock shine
skunks spray abstract into the air
cows burp as if practising
the name of Francis Ponge.
His drunk state wants the mesh of place.
Ludwig of Bavaria's Roof Garden—
glass plants, iron parrots
Venus Grottos, tarpaulins of Himalaya.
By the kitchen sink he tells someone
from now on I will drink only landscapes
– here, pour me a cup of Spain.

Opens the gate and stumbles
blood like a cassette through the body
away from the lights, unbuttoning,
this desire to be riverman.

Tentatively
              he recalls
his drunk invitation to the river.
He has steered the awesome car
past sugarbush to the blue night water

and steps out
speaking to branches
and the gulp of toads.
Subtle applause of animals.
A snake leaves a path
like temporary fossil.
                        He falls
back onto the intricacies
of gearshift and steering wheel
alive as his left arm
which now departs out of the window
trying to tug passing sumac
pine   bush   tamarack
into the car
                to the party.
Drunkenness opens his arms like a gate
and over the car invisible insects
ascend out of the beams like meteorite
crushed dust of the moon
    . . . he waits for the magic star called Lorca.

On the front lawn a sheet
tacked across a horizontal branch.
A projector starts a parade
of journeys, landscapes, relatives,
friends leaping out within pebbles of water
caught by the machine as if creating rain.

Later when wind frees the sheet
and it collapses like powder in the grass
pictures fly without target
and howl their colours over Southern Ontario
clothing burdock
rhubarb a floating duck.
Landscapes and stories
flung into branches
and the dog walks under the hover of the swing
beam of the projection bursting in his left eye.

The falling sheet the star of Lorca swoops
someone gets up and heaves his glass
into the vegetable patch
towards the slow stupid career of beans.

This is the hour
when dead men sit
and write each other.
          'Concerning the words we never said
          during morning hours of the party
          there was glass under my bare feet
          laws of the kitchen were broken
          and each word moved
          in my mouth like muscle . . . '

This is the hour for sudden journeying.
                    Cervantes accepts
a 17th Century invitation
from the Chinese Emperor.
Schools of Chinese-Spanish Linguistics!
Rivers of the world meet!
And here
ducks dressed in Asia
pivot on foreign waters.

At 4 a.m. he wakes in the sheet
that earlier held tropics in its whiteness.
The invited river flows through the house
into the kitchen up
stairs, he awakens and moves within it.
In the dim light
he sees the turkish carpet under water,
low stools, glint
of piano pedals, even a sleeping dog
whose dreams may be of rain.

It is a river he has walked elsewhere
now visiting moving with him at the hip
to kitchen where a friend sleeps in a chair
head on the table his grip
still round a glass, legs underwater.

He wants to relax
and give in to the night
fall horizontal and swim
to the back kitchen where his daughter sleeps.
He wishes to swim
to each of his family and gaze
at their underwater dreaming
this magic chain of bubbles.
Wife, son, household guests, all
comfortable in clean river water.

He is aware that for hours
there has been no conversation,
tongues have slid to stupidity on alcohol
sleeping mouths are photographs of yells.

He stands waiting, the sentinel,
shambling back and forth, his anger
and desire against the dark
which, if he closes his eyes,
will lose them all.

            The oven light
shines up through water at him
a bathysphere   a ghost ship
and in the half drowned room

the crickets like small pins
begin to tack down
the black canvas of this night,
begin to talk their hesitant
gnarled epigrams to each other
across the room.
                    Creak and echo.
Creak and echo. With absolute clarity
he knows where he is.

Tin Roof

She hesitated. 'Are you being romantic now?'
'I'm trying to tell you how I feel without
exposing myself. You know what I mean?'

ELMORE LEONARD

*

You stand still for three days
for a piece of wisdom
and everything falls to the right place

or wrong place

          You speak
      don't know whether
seraph or bitch
flutters at your heart

and look through windows
for cue cards
blazing in the sky.
             The solution.
This last year I was sure
I was going to die

*

The geography of this room   I know so well
tonight   I could rise in the dark
sit at the table   and write without light.
I am here in the country of warm rains.
A small cabin – a glass, wood,
tin bucket on the Pacific Rim.

        Geckoes climb
the window to peer in,
and all day the tirade pale blue waves
touch the black shore of volcanic rock

and fall to pieces here

*

How to arrive at this
drowning
on the edge of sea

(How to drive
the Hana Road, he said—
one hand on the beer
one hand on your thigh
and one eye for the road)

Waves leap to this cliff all day
and in the evening lose
their pale blue

he rises from the bed
as wind from three directions
falls, takes his place
on the peninsula of sheets
which also loses colour

stands in the loose green kimono
by a large window and gazes

through gecko
past the deadfall
into sea,

the unknown magic he loves
throws himself into

the blue heart

*

Tell me
all you know
about bamboo

growing wild, green
growing up into soft arches
in the temple ground

the traditions

driven through hands
through the heart
during torture

and most of all

                    this

small bamboo pipe
not quite horizontal
that drips
every ten seconds
to a shallow bowl

I love this
being here
not a word
just the faint
fall of liquid
the boom of an iron buddhist bell
in the heart rapid
as ceremonial bamboo

*

A man buying wine
Rainier beer at the store
would he be satisfied with this?
Cold showers, electric skillet,
Red River on tv
Oh he could be

(Do you want
            to be happy and write?)

He happens to love the stark
luxury of this place
– no armchairs, a fridge of beer and mangoes

        Precipitation.

To avoid a story   The refusal to move

All our narratives of sleep
a mild rumble to those inland

            Illicit pockets of
            the kimono

Heart like a sleeve

*

The cabin
       its tin roof
a wind run radio
catches the noise of the world.
He focuses on the gecko
almost transparent body
how he feels now
everything passing through him like light.
In certain mirrors
he cannot see himself at all.
He is joyous and breaking down.
The tug over the cliff.
What protects him
is the warmth in the sleeve

that is all, really

*

We go to the stark places of the earth
and find moral questions everywhere

Will John Wayne and Montgomery Clift
take their cattle to Missouri or Kansas?

Tonight I lean over the Pacific
and its blue wild silk
ringed by creatures
who
    tchick tchick tchick
my sudden movement
who say nothing else.

There are those who are in
and there are those who look in

Tiny leather toes
hug the glass

*

On the porch
thin ceramic
chimes

      ride wind
off the Pacific

bells of the sea

      I do not know
the name of large orange flowers
which thrive on salt air
lean half drunk
against the steps

Untidy banana trees
thick moss on the cliff
and then the plunge
to black volcanic shore

It is impossible to enter the sea here
except in a violent way

      How we have moved
from thin ceramic

to such destruction

*

All night
        the touch

of wave on volcano.

There was the woman
who clutched my hair
like a shaken child.
The radio whistles
round a lost wave length.

All night slack-key music
and the bird whistling *duino*
duino, words and music
entangled in pebble
ocean static.
The wild sea and her civilization
the League of the Divine Wind
and traditions of death.

        Remember
those women in movies
who wept into the hair
of their dead men?

*

Going up stairs
I hang my shirt
on the stiff
ear of an antelope

Above the bed
         memory
restless green bamboo
         the distant army
assembles wooden spears

her feet braced
on the ceiling
sea in the eye

Reading the article
an 1825 report *Physiologie du Gout*
on the artificial growing of truffles
speaks
         of 'vain efforts
and deceitful promises,'
commandments of culinary art

Good
'morning to your body
hello nipple
and appendix scar like a letter
of too much passion
from a mad Mexican doctor

All this noise at your neck!

heart clapping
like green bamboo

      this earring
    which
has flipped over
   and falls
      into the pool of your ear

The waves against black stone
that was a thousand year old
burning red river
could not reach us

*

Cabin

'hana'

      this *flower* of wood
in which we rose
out of the blue sheets
you thin as horizon
reaching for lamp or book
my shirt

      hungry
for everything about the other

here we steal places to stay
as we steal time
      never too proud to beg,
even if we never
see the other's grin and star again

there is nothing resigned
in this briefness
we swallow complete

I will know everything here

          this cup
             balanced on my chest
          my eye witnessing the petal
          drop away from its order,
          your arm

for ever

precarious in all our fury

*

Every place has its own wisdom. Come.
Time we talked about the sea,
the long waves
                    'trapped around islands'

*

There are maps now whose portraits
have nothing to do with surface

Remember the angels, floating compasses
– Portolan atlases so complex
we looked down and never knew
which was earth which was sea?
The way birds the colour of prairie
confused by the sky
flew into the earth
(Remember those women
who claimed dead miners
the colour of the coal they drowned in)

The bathymetric maps startle.
Visions of the ocean floor
troughs, naked blue deserts,
Ganges Cone, the Mascarene Basin

so one is able now
in ideal situations
to plot a stroll
to new continents
'doing the Berryman walk'

And beneath the sea
there are
these giant scratches
of pain
the markings of
some perfect animal
who has descended
burying itself
under the glossy
ballroom

or they have to do with ascending,
what we were, the earth creatures
longing for horizon.
I know one thing
our sure non-sliding
civilized feet
our small leather shoes
did not make them

(Ah you should be happy and write)

I want the passion
which puts your feet on the ceiling
this fist
to smash forward

take this silk
          somehow *Ah*
out of the rooms of poetry

(Listen, solitude, X wrote,
is not an absolute,
it is just a resting place)

listen   in the end
the pivot from angel to witch
depends on small things
this animal, the question
are you happy?

No I am not happy

lucky though

*

Rainy Night Talk

Here's to
the overlooked
nipples of Spain
          brown Madrid aureoles
kneecaps of Ohio girls
kneeling in the palms of men
waiting to be thrown high
into the clouds
of a football stadium

          Here's to
the long legged
woman from Kansas
whispering good morning at 5,
          dazed
in balcony moonlight

All that drizzle the night before
walking walking through the rain
slam her car door
and wrote my hunger out, the balcony
like an entrance
to a city of suicides.

Here's to the long legs
driving home
in more and more rain
weaving like a one-sided
lonely conversation
over the mountains

And what were you
carrying? in your head
that night Miss
Souri? Miss Kansas?

while I put my hands
sweating
on the cold
window
on the edge
of the trough of this city?

*

Breaking down after logical rules
couldn't be the hit and run driver
I wanted Frank Sinatra
I was thinking blue pyjamas
I was brought up on movies and song!

I could write my suite of poems
for Bogart   drunk
six months after the departure at Casablanca.
I see him lying under the fan
at the Slavyansky Bazar Hotel
and soon he will see the truth
the stupidity of his gesture
he'll see it in the space
between the whirling metal

                Stupid fucker
he says to himself, stupid fucker
and knocks the bottle
leaning against his bare stomach
onto the sheet. Gin stems
out like a four leaf clover.
I used to be lucky he says
I had white suits black friends
who played the piano . . .
                          and that
was a movie I saw just once.

What about Burt Lancaster
limping away at the end of *Trapeze*?
Born in 1943. And I saw that six times.
(I grew up knowing I could never fly)

That's me. You. Educated
at the *Bijou*. And don't ask me
about my interpretation of 'Madame George.'
That's a nine minute song
a two hour story

So how do we discuss
the education of our children?
Teach them to be romantics
to veer towards the sentimental?
Toss them into the air like Tony Curtis
and make 'em do the triple somersault
through all these complexities
and commandments?

*

Oh, Rilke, I want to sit down calm like you
or pace the castle, avoiding the path of the cook, Carlo,
who believes down to his turnip soup
that you speak in the voice of the devil.
I want the long lines my friend spoke of
that bamboo which sways muttering
like wooden teeth in the slim volume I have
with its childlike drawing of Duino Castle.
I have circled your book for years
like a wave combing
the green hair of the sea
kept it with me, your name
a password in the alley.
I always wanted poetry to be that
but this solitude brings no wisdom
just two day old food in the fridge,
certain habits you would not approve of.
If I said all of your name now
it would be the movement
of the tide you soared over
so your private angel
could become part of a map.

I am too often busy with things
I wish to get away from, and I want
the line to move slowly now, slow
-ly like a careful drunk across the street
no cars in the vicinity
but in his fearful imagination.
How can I link your flowing name
to geckoes or a slice of octopus?
Though there are Rainier beer cans,
magically, on the windowsill.

And still your lovely letters
January 1912 near Trieste.
The car you were driven in
'at a snail's pace'
through Provence. Wanting
'to go into chrysalis . . .
to live by the heart and nothing else.'
Or your guilt—
                    'I howl at the moon
                    with all my heart
                    and put the blame
                    on the dogs'

I can see you sitting down
the suspicious cook asleep
so it is just you
and the machinery of the night
that foul beast that sucks and drains
leaping over us sweeping our determination
away with its tail. Us and the coffee,
all the small charms we invade it with.

As at midnight we remember the colour
of the dogwood flower growing
like a woman's sex outside the window.
I wanted poetry to be walnuts
in their green cases
but now it is the sea
and we let it drown us,
and we fly to it released
by giant catapults
of pain loneliness deceit and vanity

Rock Bottom

O lady hear me. I have no

other
voice left.

ROBERT CREELEY

*

2 a.m.   The moonlight
in the kitchen

Will this be
testamentum porcelli?
Unblemished art and truth
whole hog   the pig's testament
what I know of passion
having written of it
seen my dog shiver
with love and disappear
crazy into trees

I want

the woman whose face
I could not believe in the moonlight
her mouth forever as horizon

and both of us
grim with situation

now
suddenly
we reside
near the delicate
heart
of Billie Holiday

*

You said, this
doesn't happen so quick
I must remind you of someone

　　　　　No,
though I am seduced
by this light, and
frantic arguments
on the porch,
I ain't subtle
you run rings
round me

　　　　but this quietness
white dress   long legs
arguing your body
away from me

and I with all the hunger
I didn't know I had

* *(Inner Tube)*

On the warm July river
head back

upside down river
for a roof

slowly paddling
towards an estuary between trees

there's a dog
learning to swim near me
friends on shore

my head
dips
back to the eyebrow
I'm the prow
on an ancient vessel,
this afternoon
I'm going down to Peru
soul between my teeth

a blue heron
with its awkward
broken backed flap
upside down

one of us is wrong

he
in his blue grey thud
thinking he knows
the blue way
out of here

or me

*   ('*The space in which we have dissolved –
does it taste of us?*')

Summer night came out of the water
climbed into my car and drove home
got out of the car still wet towel round me
opened the gate and walked to the house

Disintegration of the spirit
no stars
leaf being eaten by moonlight

The small creatures who are blind
who travel with the aid
of petite white horns
take over the world

Sound of a moth

The screen door in its suspicion
allows nothing in, as I allow nothing in.
The raspberries my son gave me
wild, cold out of the fridge, a few I put
in my mouth, some in my shirt pocket
and forgot

I sit here
in a half dark kitchen
the stain at my heart
caused by this gift

* *(Saturday)*

The three trunks
of the walnut

the ceremonial ducks
who limbo under the fence
and creep up the lawn

Apple tree   Blue and white house
I know this is beautiful

I wished to write today
about small things
that might persuade me
out of my want

The lines I read
about 'cowardice' and 'loyalty'
I don't know
if this is drowning
or coming up for air

          At night
I give you my hand
like a corpse
out of the water

*   *(Insomnia)*

Night and its forces
step through the picket gate
from the blue bush
to the kitchen

Everywhere it moves
and we cannot sleep we cannot sleep
we damn the missionaries
their morals thin as stars
we find ourselves
within the black
circus of the fly
all night long
his sandpaper
tabasco leg

The dog sleepwalks
into the cupboard
into the garden and heart attacks
hello
I've had a dog dream
wake up and cannot find
my long ears

Nicotine   caffeine
hungry bodies
could put us to sleep
but nothing puts us to sleep

*

How many windows have I broken?
And doors and lamps, and last month
a tumbler I smashed into a desk

then stood over the sink
digging out splinters
with an awkward left hand
I have beaten my head with stones
pieces of fence
tried to tear out my eyes
these are not exaggerations
they were acts when words failed
the way surgeons
hammer hearts gone still

now this
small parallel pain
in my finger
the invisible thing inside
circling
       glass
       on its voyage out
       to the heart

*   *(After Che-King, 11th Century BC)*

If you love me and think only of me
lift your robe and ford the river Chen

catch
        'the floating world'
8.52 from Chicago

lift your skirt
through customs,

kiss me in the parking lot

* *('La Belle Romance')*

Another deep night
with the National Enquirer

silence

like the unseen
arms of a bat

the book
falls open
to sadness
– dead flowers, dead
horses who carried
lovers to a meeting

On my last walk
through the kitchen
I see it

     I lift
huge arms of a cobweb
out of the air
and carry its Y
slowly to the porch
as if alive

as if it was a wounded bird
or some terrible camouflaged insect
that could damage children

*

The distance between us
and then this small map
of stars
          a concentrated
ocean of the night

when lovers worship heavens
they are worshipping
a lack of distance

my brother the moon
the lofty mattress
of nebula,
rash and spray of love

            It is all
as close as my palm
on your body

                    so you
among pillows and moonlight
look up, search
for the jewellery
bathing in darkness

satellite hunger, remote control,
'the royal we'

            and find
your own dark hand

*

What were the names of the towns
we drove into and through

       stunned   lost

having drunk our way
up vineyards
and then Hot Springs
boiling out the drunkenness

What were the names
I slept through
      my head
on your thigh
hundreds of miles
of blackness entering the car

        All this
        darkness and stars
but now
under the Napa Valley night
a star arch of dashboard
the ripe grape moon
we are together
and I love this muscle

I love this muscle
that tenses

      and joins
the accelerator
to my cheek

*(The linguistic war between
men and women)*

And sometimes
I think
women in novels are too
controlled by the adverb.
As they depart
a perfume of description

'She rose from the table
and left her shoe
behind, *casually*'

'Let's keep our minds
clear, she said drunkenly,'
the print hardly dry
on words like that

My problem tonight
is this landscape.
Like the sanskrit lover
who sees breasts in the high clouds,
testicles on the riverbed
('The soldiers left their balls
behind, crossing into Bangalore
she said, mournfully')

Every leaf bends
I can put my hand
into various hollows, the dogs
lick their way up the ditch
swallow the scent
of whatever they eat

Always wanted to own
a movie theatre
called 'The Moonlight'

What's playing at *The Moonlight*
she asked
leafily

Men never trail away.
They sweat adjective.
'She fell into
his unexpected arms.'
He mixes a 'devious' drink.
He spills his maddened seed
onto the lettuce—

* *(Real life)*

In real life
men talk about art
women judge men

In the Queen Street tavern
3 p.m. the only one busy
is the waitress
who reads a book a day

Hour of the afternoon soaps

Accusations
which hide the trap
door of tomorrow's guilt.
Men bursting into bedrooms
out of restaurants.
Everyone talks on phones
to the lover's brother
or the husband's mistress

My second beer
my fifth cigarette
the only thing more
confusing venomous
than real life
is this hour of the soaps
where nobody smokes
and nobody talks about art

I've woken in thick
households
all my life
but can nightmare myself
into this future—
last spring I sat here
Sunday Morning
as bachelor drunks
came in, eyes
in prayer to the Billy Graham Show

The pastel bar
grey colours of the tv
this is where people come
after the second failure of redemption

Ramon Fernandez,
                    tell me
what port you
bought that tattoo

*

Midnight dinner at the *Vesta Lunch*

Here there is nothing
I have taken from you
so I begin with memory
as old songs do

              in this café
against the night

in this villa refrain
where we collect the fragment
no longer near us
to make ourselves whole

             your bright eyes
in a greek bar, the way
you wear your hat

*

I have always
been afflicted
by angular
small breasted
women
from the mid-west,

knew this was true
the minute I met you

*

Repetition of midnight
Every creature doth sleep
But us

and the fanatics

              I want
the roulette of the lightning bolt
to decide all

On this suburban street
the skate-boarder rolls
surrounded by the seeming
hiss of electricity
                    unlit
I see him through the trees
up Ptarmigan
              a thick sweater
for the late September night

I am unable to make anything of this
who are these words for

Even the dog
curls away
into himself
the only one to know your name

*

I write about you
as if I own you
which I do not.
As you can say of nothing
this is mine.

When we rise
the last hug
no longer belongs,
is your fiction
or my story.
Mulch for the future.

Whether we pass
through each other
like pure arrows
or fade into rumour
I write down now
a fiction of your arm

or of that afternoon
in Union Station
when we both were lost
pain falling free
the speed of tears
under the Grand Rotunda
as we disappeared
rose from each other

you and your arrow
taking just
what you fled through

I will never let a chicken
into my life
but I have let you
though you squeezed in
through a screen door
the way some chickens do

I would never let chickens
influence my character
but like them good sense
scatters at your entrance
– 'poetic skill,' 'duty,'
under the fence

Your lean shoulders
studied with greyhounds.
Such ball and socket joints
I've seen only in diagrams
on the cover of *Scientific American*.
I've let greyhounds
into my vicinity
– noses, paws, ribcages
against my arm, I admit
a weakness
for reluctant modesty.
I could spend days lying on the ground
seeing the world with the perspective of snails
stumbling the small territory of obsessions
this leaf and grain of you,
could attempt the epic
journey over your shoulder.

When you were a hotel gypsy
delirious by windows
waving your arms
and singing over the parking lots
I learned from the foolish oyster
and stepped out.
So here I am
saying see this
look what I found
when I opened myself up
before death before the world,
look at this blue eye
this socket in her waving arm
these wonders.

In the night busy as snails
in wet chlorophyll apartments
we enter each other's shells
the way humans at such times
wish to enter mouths of lovers,

sleeping like the rumour of pearl
in the embrace of oyster.

I have never let spectacles into my life
and now I am walking past
where I could see.
Here,
        where the horizon was

* (*The desire under the Elms Motel*)

how I attempted seduction
with a select and
careful playing of
The McGarrigle Sisters

how you seduced me
stereophonically   the laugh

the nose   ankle   nature

       repartee   the knee

your sad determination   letters

the earring

              that falls

              'hey love—

              you forgot your glove'

*

Speaking to you
this hour
these days when
I have lost the feather of poetry
and the rains
of separation
surround us tock
tock like *Go* tablets

Everyone has learned
to move carefully

'Dancing' 'laughing' 'bad taste'
is a memory
a tableau behind trees of law

In the midst of love for you
my wife's suffering
anger in every direction
and the children wise
as tough shrubs
but they are not tough
– so I fear
how anything can grow from this

all the wise blood
poured from little cuts
down into the sink

this hour it is not
your body I want
but your quiet company

*

Dentists disguise their own bad teeth
barbers go bald, foolish birds
travel to one particular tree.
They pride themselves
on focus.
Poets cannot spell.
Everyone claims abstinence.

Reading Neruda to a class
reading his lovely old
curiosity about all things
I am told this is the first time
in months I seem happy.
Jealous of his slide
through complexity.
All afternoon I keep
stepping into his pocket

        whispering
instruct and delight me

(These back alleys)

for Daphne

In '64 you moved
and where was I?
– somewhere and married.
(In '64 everybody got married)

Whatever we are now we were then.
Some days those maps collide
falling into future land.
It seems for hours
we have sat in your car,
almost valentine's day,
I've got a plane to meet and I
hold your rose for you.
This talking
like a slow dance,
the sharing of earphones.

Since I got separated
I cannot hold
my brain in my arms anymore.
Sitting in the back alley
this new mapping, hello
to the terra nova.
Now we watch each other
in our slow walks towards
and out of everything
we wanted to know in '64

*

And for George moonlight
became her. Curious. After years of wit
he saw it enter her and believed,
singing love songs in the back seat.

Three of us drive downtown
in our confusions

goodbye to the hills of the 30's

Sinned, torn apart, how do each of us
share our hearts

and George still 'hearty,' bad jokes
scattering to the group,
does not converse, but he sings the heartbreakers
badly and precisely in the back seat

so we moon, we tough

*

Kissing the stomach
kissing your scarred
skin boat. History
is what you've travelled on
and take with you

We've each had our stomachs
kissed by strangers
to the other

and as for me
I bless everyone
who kissed you here

* *(Ends of the Earth)*

　　　For you I have slept
like an arrow in the hall
pointing towards your wakefulness
in other time zones

　　　And wary
piece by piece
we put each other together
　　　　　　your past
that of one who has walked
through fifteen strange houses
in order to be here

the charm of Wichita
gunmen in your bones
　　　the 19th century
strolling like a storm
through your long body

that history I read in comic books
and on the flickering screen
when I was thirteen

Now we are cats-cradled
in the Pacific
how does one avoid this?
Go to the ends of the earth?
The loose moon follows

　　　　　Wet moonlight
　　　　　recalls childhood

the long legged daughter
            the stars
of Wichita in the distance

midnight and hugging
against her small chest
the favourite book,
Goodnight Moon

under the covers she
reads its courtly order
its list of farewells
to everything

            We grow less complex
We reduce ourselves   The way lovers
have their small cheap charms
silver lizard,
a stone

Ancient customs
that grow from dust
            swirled out
from prairie into tropic

Strange how the odours meet

How, however briefly, bedraggled
history
        focuses

Skin Boat

'A sheet of water near your breasts
where I can sink
like a stone'

PAUL ELUARD

HER HOUSE

Because she has lived alone, her house is the product of nothing
but herself and necessity. The necessity of growing older and
raising children. Others drifted into her life, in and out and
they have changed her, added things, but I have never been
into a home that is a revelation of character and time as much
as hers. It contains those she knows and has known and she
has distilled all of her journey. When I first met her I saw
nothing but her, and now, as she becomes familiar, I recognize
the small customs.

The problem for her is leaving. She says, 'Last night I was
listening to everything I know so well, and I imagined what
if I woke up in a year's time and there were different trees.'
Streets, the weight of sea air, certain birds who recognize your
shrubbery, that too holds you, allows a freedom of habit, is a
house.

Everything here is alien to me but you. And your room like a
grey well, your coat hangers above the laundry machine where
you hang the semi-damp clothes so you do not have to iron
them, the green grey walls of wood, the secret drawer which
you opened after you knew me two years to show me the ancient
Japanese pens. All this I love. Though I carry my own
landscape in me and my three bags. But this has become your
skin, and as you leave you recognize this.

On certain evenings, when I have not bothered to put on lights,
I hit my knees on low bookcases where they should not be.
But you shift your hip easily, habitually, around them as you
pass by carrying laundry or books. When you can move
through a house blindfolded it belongs to you. You are moving
like blood calmly within your own body. It is only recently
that I am able to wake beside you and without looking, almost
in a dream, put out my hand and know exactly where your
shoulder or your heart will be – you in your specific posture in
this bed of yours that we share. And at times this has seemed
to be knowledge. As if you were a blueprint of your house.

THE CINNAMON PEELER

If I were a cinnamon peeler
I would ride your bed
and leave the yellow bark dust
on your pillow.

Your breasts and shoulders would reek
you could never walk through markets
without the profession of my fingers
floating over you. The blind would
stumble certain of whom they approached
though you might bathe
under rain gutters, monsoon.

Here on the upper thigh
at this smooth pasture
neighbour to your hair
or the crease
that cuts your back. This ankle.
You will be known among strangers
as the cinnamon peeler's wife.

I could hardly glance at you
before marriage
never touch you
– your keen nosed mother, your rough brothers.
I buried my hands
in saffron, disguised them
over smoking tar,
helped the honey gatherers . . .

When we swam once
I touched you in water
and our bodies remained free,
you could hold me and be blind of smell.
You climbed the bank and said

                    this is how you touch other women
the grass cutter's wife, the lime burner's daughter.
And you searched your arms
for the missing perfume

                    and knew

            what good is it
to be the lime burner's daughter
left with no trace
as if not spoken to in the act of love
as if wounded without the pleasure of a scar.

You touched
your belly to my hands
in the dry air and said
I am the cinnamon
peeler's wife. Smell me.

WOMEN LIKE YOU

the communal poem – Sigiri Graffiti, 5th century

They do not stir
these ladies of the mountain
do not give us
the twitch of eyelids

                The king is dead

They answer no one
take the hard
rock as lover.
Women like you
make men pour out their hearts

               'Seeing you I want `
               no other life'

               'The golden skins have
               caught my mind'

who came here
out of the bleached land
climbed this fortress
to adore the rock
and with the solitude of the air
behind them
           carved an alphabet
whose motive was perfect desire

wanting these portraits of women
to speak
and caress

Hundreds of small verses
by different hands
became one
habit of the unrequited

Seeing you
I want no other life
and turn around
to the sky
and everywhere below
jungle, waves of heat
secular love

Holding the new flowers
a circle of
first finger and thumb
which is a window

to your breast

pleasure of the skin
earring   earring
curl
of the belly
                and then
stone mermaid
stone heart
dry as a flower
on rock
you long eyed women

the golden
drunk swan breasts
lips
the long long eyes

we stand against the sky

I bring you

a flute
from the throat
of a loon

so talk to me
of the used heart

THE RIVER NEIGHBOUR

All these rumours. You lodge in the mountains
of Hang-chou, a cabin in Portland township,
or in Yüeh-chou for sure

the dust from my marriage
wasted our clear autumn

This month the cactus
under the rains

while you lounge with my children
by the creek snakes, the field asparagus

Across the universe
each room I lit
was a dark garden, I held
nothing but the lamp

this letter paints me
transparent as I am

One dead bird in the hall
conversation of the water-closets
company of the leaf on the stairs

I pass her often

Moon   leaf   memory of asparagus
I find her earrings
at the foot of curtainless windows
In the kitchen
salt fills the body
of an RCA Victor dog

Let us nose our way
next year with the spring waters
and search for each other
somewhere in the east

TO A SAD DAUGHTER

All night long the hockey pictures
gaze down at you
sleeping in your tracksuit.
Belligerent goalies are your ideal.
Threats of being traded
cuts and wounds
– all this pleases you.
O my god! you say at breakfast
reading the sports page over the Alpen
as another player breaks his ankle
or assaults the coach.

When I thought of daughters
I wasn't expecting this
but I like this more.
I like all your faults
even your purple moods
when you retreat from everyone
to sit in bed under a quilt.
And when I say 'like'
I mean of course 'love'
but that embarrasses you.
You who feel superior to black and white movies
(coaxed for hours to see *Casablanca*)
though you were moved
by *Creature from the Black Lagoon*.

One day I'll come swimming
beside your ship or someone will
and if you hear the siren
listen to it. For if you close your ears
only nothing happens. You will never change.

I don't care if you risk
your life to angry goalies
creatures with webbed feet.
You can enter their caves and castles
their glass laboratories. Just
don't be fooled by anyone but yourself.

This is the first lecture I've given you.
You're 'sweet sixteen' you said.
I'd rather be your closest friend
than your father. I'm not good at advice
you know that, but ride
the ceremonies
until they grow dark.

Sometimes you are so busy
discovering your friends
I ache with a loss
– but that is greed.
And sometimes I've gone
into *my* purple world
and lost you.

One afternoon I stepped
into your room. You were sitting
at the desk where I now write this.
Forsythia outside the window
and sun spilled over you
like a thick yellow miracle
as if another planet
was coaxing you out of the house
– all those possible worlds! –
and you, meanwhile, busy with mathematics.

I cannot look at forsythia now
without loss, or joy for you.
You step delicately
into the wild world
and your real prize will be
the frantic search.
Want everything. If you break
break going out not in.
How you live your life I don't care
but I'll sell my arms for you,
hold your secrets for ever.

If I speak of death
which you fear now, greatly,
it is without answers,
except that each
one we know is
in our blood.
Don't recall graves.
Memory is permanent.
Remember the afternoon's
yellow suburban annunciation.
Your goalie
in his frightening mask
dreams perhaps
of gentleness.

ALL ALONG THE MAZINAW

Later the osprey

falling towards
only what he sees

the messenger heron
warning of our progress
up Mud Lake

a paddle is
stranger
to what it heaves out of the way

Wherever you go
within a silence
is witnessed,
                touches.
Everything aware
of alteration but you.
Creatures who veer. The torn leaf
descending into marsh gas
into an ancient breath.

In bony rapids
rock gazed up
with the bright paint
of previous canoes.

But now, you, *c'est là*,
with the clear river water heart
the rock who floats
on her own deep reflection.
Female rock. Limb. Holes of hunger
we climb into and disappear.

One hour in the arms of the Mazinaw.

Those things we don't know we love
we love harder.
                    Tanned face
stern rock   the rock lolling
memorized by the Algonquin
Mohawk lovers. Mineral eye.

O yes I saw your dear sisters too
before this afternoon's passion
those depot creek nights when they
unpacked their breasts
serious and full of the fever of loon
for whoever stumbled
young onto the august
country waters.

PACIFIC LETTER

to Stan of Depot Creek, old friend, pal o'mine

Now I remember that you rebuilt my chicken coop
north of the farmhouse along the pasture fence
with fresh pine from Verona.
In autumn you hid a secret message under floorboards
knowing we would find it in spring.
A fanciful message. Carved with care.
As you carved you imagined the laughing.
We both know the pleasures art and making bring.

And in summer we lounged for month on month
letting slide the publishers and English Departments
who sent concerned letters that slept in the red mailbox.
Men and women came drifting in
from the sea and from the west border
and with them there was nothing at cross purpose.
They made nothing of mountain crossing
to share that fellowship.
The girls danced because
their long sleeves would not keep still
and I, drunk, went to sleep among field rocks.
We spoke out desires without regret.
Then you returned to the west of the province
and I to the south.

After separation had come to its worst
we met and travelled the Mazinaw with my sons
through all the thirty-six folds of that creature river
into the valley of bright lichen,
green rice beds, marble rock, and at night
slept under croaking pine.
The spirit so high it was all over the heavens!

And at Depot Creek we walked
for a last time down river
to a neighbour's southern boundary
past the tent where you composed verses
past the land where I once lived
the water about it clear in my memory as blue jade.
Then you and your wife sang back and forth
in the mosquito filled cabin under the naphtha.
The muskrat, listening at the edge,
heard our sound – guitars and lone violin
whose weavings seduced us with a sadness.

The canoe brushed over open lake
hearing the lighted homes
whose laughter eliminated the paddle
and the loon stumbled
up sudden into the air beside the boat
shocked us awake and disappeared
leaving a ripple that slid the moon away.
And before the last days in August
we scattered like stars and rain.

And I think now that this
is what we are to each other,
friends busy with their own distance
who reappear now and then alongside.
As once you could not believe
I had visited the town of your youth
where you sat in your room
perfecting *Heartbreak Hotel*
that new place to 'dwell' – that
gentle word in the midst of angry song.

All this comes to an end.
During summer evenings
I miss your company.
Things we clung to

stay on the horizon
and we become the loon
on his journey
a lone tropical taxi
to confused depth and privacy.

At such times – no talking
no conclusion in the heart.

I buy postage
                    seal this

and send it a thousand miles, thinking.

A DOG IN SAN FRANCISCO

Sitting in an empty house
with a dog from the Mexican Circus!
O Daisy, embrace is my only pleasure.
Holding and hugging my friends. Education.
A wave of eucalyptus. Warm granite.
These are the things I have in my heart.
Heart and skills, there's nothing else.

I usually don't like small dogs but you
like midwestern women take over the air.
You leap into the air and pivot
a diver going up! You are known
to open the fridge and eat when you wish
you can roll down car windows and step out
you know when to get off the elevator.

I always wanted to be a dog
but I hesitated
for I thought they lacked certain skills.
Now I want to be a dog.

TRANSLATIONS OF MY POSTCARDS

the peacock means order
the fighting kangaroos mean madness
the oasis means I have struck water

positioning of the stamp – the despot's head
horizontal, or 'mounted policemen',
mean political danger

the false date means I
am not where I should be

when I speak of the weather
I mean business

a blank postcard says
I am in the wilderness

7 OR 8 THINGS I KNOW ABOUT HER–
A STOLEN BIOGRAPHY

The Father's Guns

After her father died they found nine guns in the house. Two
in his clothing drawers, one under the bed, one in the glove
compartment of the car, etc. Her brother took their mother out
onto the prairie with a revolver and taught her to shoot.

The Bird

For a while in Topeka parrots were very popular. Her father
was given one in lieu of a payment and kept it with him at
all times because it was the fashion. It swung above him in the
law office and drove back with him in the car at night. At
parties friends would bring their parrots and make them
perform what they had been taught: the first line from *Twelfth
Night*, a bit of Italian opera, cowboy songs, or a surprisingly
good rendition of Russ Colombo singing 'Prisoner of Love'. Her
father's parrot could only imitate the office typewriter, along
with the *ching* at the end of each line. Later it broke its neck
crashing into a bookcase.

The Bread

Four miles out of Topeka on the highway – the largest electrical
billboard in the State of Kansas. The envy of all Missouri. It
advertised bread and the electrical image of a knife cut slice
after slice. These curled off endlessly. 'Meet you at the bread,'
'See you at the loaf,' were common phrases. Aroused couples
would park there under the stars on the open night prairie.
Virtue was lost, 'kissed all over by every boy in Wichita'. Poets,
the inevitable visiting writers, were taken to see it, and it
hummed over the seductions in cars, over the nightmares of
girls in bed. Slice after slice fell towards the earth. A feeding
of the multitude in this parched land on the way to Dorrance,
Kansas.

First Criticism

She is two weeks old, her mother takes her for a drive. At the gas station the mechanic is cleaning the windshield and watches them through the glass. Wiping his hands he puts his head in the side window and says, 'Excuse me for saying this but I know what I'm talking about – that child has a heart condition.'

Listening In

Overhear her in the bathroom, talking to a bug: 'I don't want you on me, honey.' 8 a.m.

Self-Criticism

'For a while there was something about me that had a dubious quality. Dogs would not take meat out of my hand. The town bully kept handcuffing me to trees.'

Fantasies

Always one fantasy. To be travelling down the street and a man in a clean white suit (the detail of 'clean' impresses me) leaps into her path holding flowers and sings to her while an invisible orchestra accompanies his solo. All her life she has waited for this and it never happens.

Reprise

In 1956 the electric billboard in Kansas caught fire and smoke plumed into a wild sunset. Bread on fire, broken glass. Birds flew towards it above the cars that circled round to watch. And last night, past midnight, her excited phone call. Her home town is having a marathon to benefit the symphony. She pays $4 to participate. A tuxedoed gentleman begins the race with a clash of cymbals and she takes off. Along the route at frequent intervals are quartets who play for her. When they stop for water a violinist performs a solo. So here she comes. And there I go, stepping forward in my white suit, with a song in my heart.

BESSIE SMITH AT ROY THOMSON HALL

At first she refused to sing.

She had applied for the one concert – that she was allowed each sabbatical – to take place in Havana. Palms! Oh Pink Walls! Cuba! she would hum to herself, dazzling within the clouds.

But here she was. Given the choice of nine Honest Ed restaurants and then hurried to Roy Thomson Hall which certainly should never have been called that.

> A long brown dress, with fringes.
> Fred Longshaw at the piano.

She opened the first set with 'Kitchen Man'. Five people left. Al Neil had flown in from Vancouver on a tip. For the next ten minutes, after people realized it really *was* Bessie Smith, the hall was filled with shouted requests. 'Any Woman's Blues', 'Down in the Dumps' . . . until she said I want to sing what I never was allowed to, because I died. And she brought the rest of the twentieth century under her wing.

She wore wings. They raised themselves with her arms each time she coaxed a phrase. Her wings would float up and fall slow like a hand held out of a car coming down against the wind, the feathers black as the Steinway. You should have been there.

During the intermission the stunned audience just sat in their seats. 'She's looking good' was one of the common remarks.

When she returned she brought out the band. They were glad to have arrived on earth, but they too had hoped for Havana. Abraham Wheat on soprano sax was there. Joe Smith on cornet was there. By midnight her voice was even better. She talked more between songs.

At 2 a.m. the band levitated. She used no microphone. Above us banners waved and danced like a multitude. She took on and caressed the songs of Jerome Kern. She asked what happened to her friend Charlie Green. And then, to her surprise, to apologize for Toronto, Charlie Green was allowed to join her. He had been found frozen in a Harlem tenement but now stepped forward shyly with his trombone. And now he and Joe Smith and Bessie Smith were alone on stage the audience quiet and the banners still and the air conditioning holding its breath. They wheeled away the Steinway. They brought out an old upright decorated with bullet holes. Al Neil was asked to sit in. She sang, 'It won't be You'.

The encore was made up of two songs. 'Weeping Willow Blues' and 'Far Away Blues'. We stood like sudden wheat. But she could not hear us. She could not see us. Then she died again.

THE CONCESSIONS

i.

Wawanosh.
            In the corn of night
surrounded by the dusty dark green
hot insects and moon
                        a star coat.

We are new and ancient here
talking through midnight's
tired arms,
letting go the newness.
I am home.
Old farmhouse, a defunct red truck
under the trees
conversation all evening
and I have nothing more to say
but this is a magic night.
Our bodies betray us, long for sleep.
Still – talk about the bear, the cause
of theatre, the first time we all met.

A yellow light falls onto the sink
and our arms lean forward
towards Elmira coffee cake.
Hello again, after Pacific months,
and I brought you a seed I never gave you
and I brought you stories and a peace I want
to give, but it is both of you
who bring comfort and friendship.

All night we are at this table.
            Tableau of faint light,
fragment of Ontario.
We would be plotting revolution in the 1830's.
And outside the same heat, old coat of stars,
the released lung of the country, and
great Ontario night beans growing
towards Goderich.
            Lone houses
betrayed by poplar
reached only by long arms
of Wawanosh concessions,
the crow of night.

            Tomorrow
will be all highway
till I get home.
Go to bed, exhausted and alone.
Go to bed with each others' minds.
I do not know what to say
about this kind of love
but I refuse to lose it.

ii.

By the outhouse and red truck
I look up towards a lit window
which seeps a yellow road into trees.
To end in the warm
glove of a maple!
A bear.
Welcome Shakespeare, Sarah Bernhardt,
someone is starting a new story.
Someone is dancing new on this
terrific ancient earth, claiming this
for mute ancestors
and their language of hands.
    The entertainers
who allow themselves long evenings
while others sleep.
The suspicious work of the community.

The town of Molesworth
which once housed a dancing cow
articulated us. As did the director
from Atwood, the fiddler from Listowel,
and the actress from Fergus, the writer from Wingham,
the mystic from Millbank.
These country hearts, a county conspiracy.
Their determined self-portraits
where alone one picks
up the pencil, begins with nothing
but these blank pages.
Let me tell you, I love them more and more
– all their night silences, their ignored dream.

In daylight the car hums. Bluevale   Seaforth
Newry   Holmesville.
The deer and flamingos, another mythology,
grace every tenth house.
This is not your home
but you are home.
                    Geraniums
in a tractor tire, horse weathervanes.
Moon over the Maitland River . . .

And so that yellow light
man or woman working inside
aware of the cricket night
cricket cricket . . . cicada? he writes, she says
to no one but the page
black hallways behind him
and ahead the windowscreen and then
the yard of yellow highway into maple
which his mind can walk out on
and dream a story
for his friends, the community

as someone once imagined
a dancing cow, a giant cheese.
The dream made name.
The gestures of the barroom
made dictionary.

iii.

When the four piece band sat stony in the Blyth Hotel
and played *Maple Sugar*, the bar got up to dance.
My shoulder banging against the women's room
to avoid flying drunk feet in their boots
that brought the cowshit in. And the bullshit
came too, through the beer and smoke.

This lady on the electric piano, the two fiddlers
and guitarist, the actors from across the street
stepping up to sing, receive stormy ovations.
The tv green and orange above us
recording grade B Hollywood, flamingo art.
And something is happening here.
Town and actors exchanging clothes.
The mechanic holds his harmonica
professionally against the mike
piercing out 'Have you ever been lonely
have you ever been blue,'
and, as the man from Lobo says,
Fuck the Renaissance
– just get me a beer.

iv.

So this midnight choir.

At 2 a.m. everyone is thrown out
and spreads onto the empty streets.
Unseen, as we step into cars,
are the bear and hawk,
who generate us.
And from the unseen sky
the crow watches
traffic light up Highway 4
then turn into unpaved
yellow concession roads.

The car bounces on a grass path
between tall corn and stops.

Light from the open car
reveals the yard.
And, as if painted onto the night,
is the yellow window
where someone, holding a mirror
is drawing a picture of herself.

RED ACCORDION–
AN IMMIGRANT SONG

How you and I talked!
Casually, and side by side,
not even cold at 4 a.m.
New Year's morning

in a double outhouse in Blyth.

Creak of trees and scrub snow.
Was it dream or true memory
this casualness, this ease of talk
after the long night of the previous year.

Nothing important said
just as now the poem
draws together such frail times.
Art steps forward as accident
like a warm breeze from Brazil.

      This whispering
as if not to awaken
what hibernates in firewood
as if not to disturb the blue night
the last memory of the year.

      So we sit
within loose walls of the poem
you and I, our friends indoors
drunk on the home-made wine.
All of us searching to discern ourselves,
the 'gift' we can give each other.
Tell this landscape.
Or the one we came from.

Polkas in a smoky midnight light.

I stepped into this new year
dancing with a small child.
Rachel, so graceful,
we bowed when the dance was over.
If I could paint this I would

                    and if writing
showed colour and incident
removed from time
                    we could be clear.

The bleak view past the door
is where we are, not what we
have made here, or become, or brought
like wolves bringing food to a lair
from another world. And this
is magic.
            Ray Bird's seven-year-old wine
– transformed! Finally made good.
I drank an early version years ago
and passed out.
                    Time collapses.
The years, the intricate
knowledge now of each other
makes love.

A yard in its scrub snow, stacked wood
brindle in the moonlight, the red truck,
a bare tree at the foot of the driveway
waving to heaven.

                    A full moon the
                    colour of night kitchen.

Ten yards away a high bonfire
(remembered from summer) lifts
its redness above the farmhouse
and the lean figures of children circle
to throw in sticks and arms off a christmas tree
as the woman in long black hair
her left foot on a stump
plays the red accordion.

And the others dance.
                    Embracing or flinging
themselves away from each other.
They bow and they look up
to full moon and white cold sky
and they *move*, even in this stilled painting.
They talk a white breath at each other.
Some appear more than once
with different partners.
We are immune to wind.
Our boots pound down the frozen earth
our children leap from and into our arms.
All of us poised and inspired by music
friendship self-made heat and the knowledge
each has chosen to come here driven for hours
over iced highways, to be here bouncing and leaping

to a reel that carried itself generations ago
north of the border, through lost towns,
settled among the strange names,
and became eventually our own

all the way from Virginia.

IN A YELLOW ROOM

There was another reason for Fats Waller to record, on May 8th, 1935, 'I'm gonna sit right down and write myself a letter.' It is for this moment, driving from Goderich towards and past Blyth, avoiding Blyth by taking the gravel concessions, four adults and a child, who have just swum in a very cold Lake Huron. His piano drips from the cassette player and we all recognize the piece but are mute. We cannot sing before he does, before he eases himself into the lyrics as if into a chair, this large man who is to die in 1943 sitting in a train in Kansas City, finally still.

He was always moving, grand on the street or the midnight taxi rides with Andy Razaf during which it is rumoured he wrote most of his songs. I have always loved him but I love him most in the company of friends. Because his body was a crowd and we desire to imitate such community. His voice staggers or is gentle behind a whimsical piano, the melody ornamental and cool as vichyssoise in that hot studio in this hot car on a late June Ontario summer day. What else of importance happened on May 8th, 1935?

The only creature I've ever met who disliked him was a nervous foxhound I had for three years. As soon as I put on Mr Waller the dog would dart from the room and hide under a bed. The dog recognized the anarchy, the unfolding of musical order, the growls and muttering, the fact that Fats Waller was talking to someone over your shoulder as well as to you. What my dog did not notice was the serenity he should have learned from. The notes as fresh as creek washed clothes.

The windows are open as we drive under dark maples that sniff up a rumour of Lake Huron. The piano energizes the hay bound into wheels, a white field of turkeys, various tributaries of the Maitland River. Does he, drunk, and carrying his tin of tomatoes – 'it feeds the body and cuts the hangover' – does he, in the midnight taxi with Razaf, imagine where the music disappears?

Where it will recur? Music and lyrics they wrote then
sold to false composers for ready cash and only later
admitting they had written 'Sunny side of the street' and 'I
can't give you anything but love' and so many of the best
songs of their time. The hidden authors on their two hour taxi
ride out of Harlem to Brooklyn and back again to Harlem,
the night heat and smells yells overheard from the streets they
passed through which they incorporated into what they were
making every texture entering this large man, a classical
organist in his youth, who strode into most experiences, hid
from his ex-wife Edith Hatchett, visiting two kinds of women,
'ladies who had pianos and ladies who did not,' and died of
bronchial pneumonia on the Acheson-Topeka and Santa Fe, a
song he did not write.

He and the orchestra of his voice have now entered the car with
us. This is his first visit to the country, though he saw it from a
train window the day before he died. Saw the heartland where
the music could disappear, the diaspora of notes, a rewinding,
a backward movement of the formation of the world, the
invention of his waltz.

WHEN YOU DRIVE THE
QUEENSBOROUGH ROADS AT MIDNIGHT

do not look at a star
or full moon. Look out for frogs.
And not the venerable ones who recline
on gravel parallel to the highway
but the foolhardy, bored on a country night
dazzled by the adventure of passing beams.

We know their type of course, local heroes
who take off their bandanas and leap naked,
night green, seduced
by the whispers of michelin.

To them we are distinct death.
I am fond of these foolish things
more than the moon.
They welcome me after absence.
One of them is my youth
still jumping into rivers
take care and beware of him.

Knowing you love this landscape
there are few rules.
Do not gaze at moons.
Nuzzle the heat in granite.
Swim toward pictographs.
Touch only reflections.

PROUST IN THE WATERS

for Scott and Krystyne

Swimming along the bar of moon
the yellow scattered sleeping
arm of the moon
               on Balsam Lake

releasing the air
              out of your mouth
the moon under your arm
tick of the brain
submerged. Tick
of the loon's heart
in the wet night thunder
                 below us
knowing its shore is the air

We love things which disappear
and are found
creatures who plummet
and become
an arrow.
To know the syllables
in a loon sentence
             intricate
shift of preposition
that signals meridian
              west   south west.
The mother tongue
a bubble caught in my beak
releasing the air
            of a language

Seeing no human in this moon storm
being naked in black water
you approach the corridor
such jewellery! Queen Anne's Lace!
and slide to fathoms.
The mouth swallows river morse
throws a sound
through the loom of liquid
against sky.

Where are you?

On the edge
of the moon bar

ESCARPMENT

He lies in bed, awake, holding her left forearm. It is 4 a.m. He turns, his eyes rough against the night. Through the window he can hear the creek – which has no name. Yesterday at noon he walked along its shallow body overhung with cedar, beside rushes, moss and watercress. A green and grey body whose intricate bones he is learning among which he stumbles and walks through in an old pair of Converse running shoes. She was further upriver investigating for herself and he exploring on his own now crawling under a tree that has uprooted and spilled. Its huge length across a section of the creek. With his left hand he holds onto the massive stump roots and slides beneath it within the white water heaving against him. Shirt wet, he follows the muscle in the water and travels fast under the tree. His dreaming earlier must have involved all this.

In the river he was looking for a wooden bridge which they had crossed the previous day. He walks confidently now, the white shoes stepping casually off logs into deep water, through gravel, and watercress which they eat later in a cheese sandwich. She chews much of it walking back to the cabin. He turns and she freezes, laughing, with watercress in her mouth. There are not many more ways he can tell her he loves her. He shows mock outrage and yells but she cannot hear him over the sound of the stumbling creek.

He loves too, as she knows, the body of rivers. Provide him with a river or a creek and he will walk along it. Will step off and sink to his waist, the sound of water and rock encasing him in solitude. The noise around them insists on silence if they are more than five feet apart. It is only later when they sit in a pool legs against each other that they can talk, their conversation roaming to include relatives, books, best friends, the history of Lewis and Clark, fragments of the past which they piece together. But otherwise this river's noise encases them and now he walks alone with its spirits, the clack and splash, the twig break, hearing only an individual noise if it occurs less than an arm's length away. He is looking, now, for a name.

It is not a name for a map – he knows the arguments of imperialism. It is a name for them, something temporary for their vocabulary. A code. He slips under the fallen tree holding the cedar root the way he holds her forearm. He hangs a moment, his body being pulled by water going down river. He holds it the same way and for the same reasons. Heart Creek? Arm River? he writes, he mutters to her in the darkness. The body moves from side to side and he hangs with one arm, deliriously out of control, still holding on. Then he plunges down, touches gravel and flakes of wood with his back the water closing over his head like a clap of gloved hands. His eyes are open as the river itself pushes him to his feet and he is already three yards down stream and walking out of the shock and cold stepping into the sun. Sun lays its crossword, litters itself, along the whole turning length of this river so he can step into heat or shadow.

He thinks of where she is, what she is naming. Near her, in the grasses, are Bladder Campion, Devil's Paintbrush, some unknown blue flowers. He stands very still and cold in the shadow of long trees. He has gone far enough to look for a bridge and has not found it. Turns upriver. He holds onto the cedar root the way he holds her forearm.

BIRCH BARK

for George Whalley

An hour after the storm on Birch Lake
the island bristles. Rock. Leaves still falling.
At this time, in the hour after lightning
we release the canoes.
Silence of water
purer than the silence of rock.
A paddle touches itself. We move
over blind mercury, feel the muscle
within the river, the blade
weave in dark water.

Now each casual word is precisely chosen
passed from bow to stern, as if
leaning back to pass a canteen.
There are echoes, repercussions of water.
We are in absolute landscape,
among names that fold in onto themselves.

To circle the island means witnessing
the blue grey dust of a heron
released out of the trees.
So the dialogue slides
nothing more than friendship
an old song we break into
not needing all the words.

We are past naming the country.
The reflections are never there
without us, without the exhaustion
of water and trees after storm.

BREEZE

for BP *Nichol*

Nowadays I listen only to duets.
Johnny Hodges and The Bean, a thin slip
of piano behind them
on this page on this stage
craft a breeze in a horn.

One friend sits back and listens
to the other. Nowadays
I want only the wild and tender
phrasing of "NightHawk,"
its air groaned out
like the breath of a lover.
Rashomon by Saxophone.

So brother and sister woke, miles apart,
in those 19th century novels you loved,
with the same wound or desire.

We sit down to clean and sharpen
the other's most personal lines
—a proposal of more, a waving dismissal
of whole stanzas—in Lethbridge in Edmonton
you stood with the breeze
in an uncomfortable Chinese restaurant
in Camrose, getting a second cup
at The Second Cup near Spadina.

I almost called you this morning
for a phone number.
Records I haven't yet returned.
Tapes you were supposed to make for me.

And across the country
tears about your death.
I always thought, someone says,
he was very good for you.
Though I still like, Barrie,
the friends who are not good for me.

Along the highway
only the duets and wind fill up my car.
I saw the scar of the jet that Sunday
trying to get you out of the sky.
Ben Webster, Coleman Hawkins.
An A and an H, a bean and a breeze.

All these twin truths

There is bright sumac, once more,
this September, along the Bayview Extension

From now on
no more solos

I tie you to me

A note on the poems

The Cinnamon Peeler contains poems that cover a twenty-five year period. They are poems that were written alongside and between other longer works such as *The Collected Works of Billy the Kid, Coming Through Slaughter, Running in the Family,* and *In the Skin of a Lion.* They cover the period from 1963, when I first started to write, to 1990.

Elimination Dance, which turns up here as an intermission, is a sort of rogue-troubadour poem that seems continually to change—a few lines get dropped and a few get added every year. It is based on those horrendous dances where a caller decides, seemingly randomly, who should not be allowed to continue dancing. So the piece (I still hesitate to call it a poem) is in the voice of a mad, and totally beyond-the-pale, announcer.

Two poems in *Secular Love,* 'The River Neighbour' and 'Pacific Letter', are based on the Rihaku-Tu Fu-Ezra Pound poems. They are not so much translations as re-locations into my landscape, with a few lines by the earlier poets making their appearance in my poem.

Most of these poems were written in Canada. A few were written in Sri Lanka. Tin Roof was written in Hawaii.

Trick with a Knife was dedicated to Kim and Quintin and Griffin. And *Secular Love* was dedicated to Linda.

MICHAEL ONDAATJE

ALSO BY MICHAEL ONDAATJE

HANDWRITING

Poems

Handwriting is Michael Ondaatje's first new book of poetry since *The Cinnamon Peeler*. It is a collection of exquisitely crafted poems of delicacy and power—poems about love, landscape, and the sweep of history set in the poet's first home, Sri Lanka. Ondaatje writes of desire and longing, the curve of a bridge against a woman's foot, the figure of a man walking through a rainstorm to a tryst. The falling away of culture is juxtaposed with an individual's sense of loss, grief, and remembrance as Ondaatje weaves a rich tapestry of images— the unburial of stone Buddhas, a family of stilt-walkers crossing a field, the pattern of teeth marks on skin drawn by a monk from memory.

Handwriting is a poetic achievement by a writer at the height of his creative powers. In it, we are reminded once again of Michael Ondaatje's unique artistry with language and of his stature as one of the finest poets writing today.

Poetry/0-375-70541-4

VINTAGE INTERNATIONAL
Available at your local bookstore, or call toll-free to order:
1-800-793-2665 (credit cards only).

ALSO BY MICHAEL ONDAATJE

THE ENGLISH PATIENT

"Sensuous, mysterious, rhapsodic, it transports the reader to another world." —*San Francisco Chronicle*

Now a major motion picture, starring Ralph Fiennes, Juliette Binoche, and Kristin Scott Thomas. During the final moments of World War II, four damaged people come together in a deserted Italian villa. As their stories unfold, a complex tapestry of image and emotion is woven, leaving them inextricably connected by the brutal circumstances of the war.

Fiction/Literature/0-679-74520-3

RUNNING IN THE FAMILY

"With a prose style equal to the voluptuousness of its subject and a sense of humor never too far away, *Running in the Family* is sheer reading pleasure." —*Washington Post Book World*

In the late 1970s, Michael Ondaatje returned to his native country of Sri Lanka. Recording his journey through the druglike heat and intoxicating fragrances of the island, Ondaatje simultaneously retraces the baroque mythology of his Dutch-Ceylonese family.

Memoir/Literature/0-679-74669-2

COMING THROUGH SLAUGHTER

"A novelist with the heart of a poet." —*Chicago Tribune*

This novel brings to life the fabulous, colorful panorama of New Orleans in the first flush of the jazz era; it is the story of Buddy Bolden, the first of the great trumpet players, some say the originator of jazz, who was a genius, a guiding spirit, and the king of that time and place.

Fiction/Literature/0-679-76785-1

ALSO AVAILABLE:

The Collected Works of Billy the Kid/Fiction/Literature/0-679-76786-X
In the Skin of a Lion/Fiction/Literature/0-679-77266-9

VINTAGE INTERNATIONAL
Available at your local bookstore, or call toll-free to order:
1-800-793-2665 (credit cards only).